FIRE OF LOVE

J.M.J. Publications
PO Box 385
Belfast
United Kingdom
Fax: (1232) 381596

His Holiness Pope Paul VI has confirmed on
October 14, 1966, the decree of the Sacred
Congregation for the propagation of the Faith,
under number 58/16 (A.A.S.), permitting the
publication of writings about supernatural
apparitions, even if they do not have a "nihil
obstat" from ecclesiastical authorities.

'Fire of Love'

1995   1st Printing (Canada) - 10,000

See back of book for the addresses of distributors

Dedication

This book is dedicated to
the Most Holy Trinity

PREFACE

Within the fellowship of God's people, **commitment to Christ** constitutes the foundation and core of the life and ministry of all believers, priests, teachers, bishops. Some are called to a discipleship in which their personal identity and faithfulness to Christ is of paramount significance, or to a distinctive calling which may represent an intensification of a close familiarity with the Risen Christ. Out of this intimate proximity and abundant dialogue, the faithful disciple is committed, under a solemn vow, to echo this unique joy. He/she is not sent to disclose a new revelation, but to re-tell and re-write anew what has been already revealed and manifested; "I find it necessary to write and to appeal to you to contend for the faith that was once for all entrusted to the saints" (Jude 3).

Fire of Love is a story written by a reminder of **The** Reminder. At this stage of history and in this particular place and situation, the reminder's name is Vassula. Her analysis is realistic. Facing the present human unbelief, disobedience to the church, false prophecy, all speaking "the language of the world", there is no time for complacency and lack of discipline. Christ wants a

i

disciplined community with disciplined faithfulness to God. Where there is faith, God works through the feeble and the powerless, but where there is no repentance and faith, the weakness is weakness. There is an urgency of time, for the intruders and "traders" of Christ are increasing the ignorance of God, perverting and undermining the grace of God, and rejecting our only Master and Lord, Jesus Christ (Jude 4). By saying: Christ is risen, one goes beyond denouncing this world. One becomes a witness to the new world which will not pass. This introduction is not meant to canonize the content and method of *Vassula's Spiritual Conversations*, nor to judge her as a skilful writer in various styles: doxological, sentimental, poetical, penitential. Rather it is to see how the two arms of God, the Son and the Spirit, (St Irenaeos about 130-2) take a disciple and do mighty works through her.

Jesus Christ taught us the Word of God, being Himself the living Logos of God. When the Jews reproached Jesus for not himself having been taught, He answered: "My teaching is not from Myself: it comes from the One who sent Me; and if anyone is prepared to do His Will, he will know whether My teaching is from God" (John 7:16). Jesus insisted on the **content** of love: "If anyone loves Me, he will keep My Word.... Those who do not love Me, do not keep My words. And My word is not My own: it is the word of the One who sent Me" (John 14:23-24). And the Good News has a certain objectivity. He refers to "My commandments", to what is written in the Book of Psalms (Luke 20:42), in the Law of Moses, in the Prophets (Luke 24:44). Jesus did not remain in the desert, but explained the passages from the Scriptures in the Temple, and in encounters on the road (Luke 24:27-32). It is precisely by His teaching that He created a circle of disciples: "Because He taught them with authority, and not like the scribes" (Matt 7:29). All His life and ministry are in "conformity" with the *oikonomia* of the God of Salvation. He was absorbed by His Father's affairs, (Luke 2:49). He went about the Holy Land but finally He turned back to Jerusalem, where His Crucifixion became His glorification.

The Risen Christ is now active in the Spirit, as becomes clear on the day of Pentecost. He needs the Spirit to communicate with us, therefore He enjoins on us: "Do not suppress My Spirit". The Spirit is the Truth, who "will teach you everything and remind you of all I have said to you" (John 14:26). The Spirit is His witness,"another witness" (John 5,6), since He will not speak as from Himself, but will say only what He has learned, and will teach you of the things to come" (John 16:13). But the Spirit is freedom, like a wind blowing where it pleases. Where there are false teachers and teaching, the Spirit repeats strictly what Jesus said. Where there are faithful disciples, the Spirit reveals the hidden jewels of God's wisdom. The Spirit will complete in us the perfect love of the Risen Christ. "Do not say that all I had to say to you has been said! Why limit me as yourself?" Jesus imparts gifts,, abilities, ministries, through the Holy Spirit. The Holy Spirit, who is present everywhere and fills all things, goes out to reach the whole world.

"For you too will be my witnesses". Here is the role of the reminders of **The** Reminder and witnesses to **The** Witness, who are not selected and appointed to an office, but blessed and anointed to testify that **Christ is Risen!** "I am free to send you new portents and fresh workers". Their quality is perfect love and loyalty, and when it is necessary Jesus Christ asks them to rewrite His message. What a lesson about the "schola" character of Christianity! The Gospel is not imposed by imperial edict, decree of a magisterium, decisions of a council, by intellectual oppression or cultural conformism. The Christian is a *scholastics* absorbed in a master-disciple colloquium and gracious mutual communications. It could be turned into conversion, renewal of mind and heart. The scholastics will then say: "I vow to remain faithful to You; this is my solemn vow. Help me to keep this vow for ever and ever". The disciple of the Master remains a student, a pupil.

Fire of Love utters a heavy word and warning for ecumenical Christianity. The symbol of " three iron bars" is true, and corresponds with the "rigidity" of Churches petrified in the sleep and lethargy of division. This is also here a matter of **commitment to Christ**. In His Message, Christ asks for some urgent "reparations", at least to celebrate Easter on a common date. Only the fire of the Spirit can melt and bend the immobile bars. If not, Jesus will reject Christians like "rotten wood". In an age when so many sectarian and fundamentalist groups retain all our attention and leave no time for remembrance of God, Christians cannot be completely deaf to the persuasion and advice of Vassula in regard to new signs of unity, here and now. There is something universal in this message, recalling that "all of you are one in Christ Jesus" (Gal 3:28).

Tradition specifies no limits to the material and medium to be used in communicating the Gospel message, requiring only that it be appropriate. The historical practice retains a strict number of teaching ministries: pastors, priests, teachers, theologians, bishops. Could we interpret Tradition as being concerned with other kinds of communication, eg. exceptional charismatic reminders? Does it provide sufficient ground for taking as comprehensive a view as possible of those who are bearers of a vision of Christ, communicating through written words, received from above? The Church then has to recognize the gifts of the faithful, to develop and integrate them into the life of the whole Body. Discerning them, restraining some and encouraging others.

The author of *Fire of Love* possesses a visible testimony of her experience through her **hands**. The task of the voice and hand of the Reminder is not a mechanical one. She has to cope with her humanity, strengths, failures and weakness. She needs to come before God in penance and prayer. She needs to be sustained by the communion of believers and saints. Her stubbornness to say "Christ is Risen" as an unceasing prayer can irritate many. She is under the scrutiny of those who are questioning the objectivity and history of her apparitions, revelation and prediction. Her strength pointing beyond herself to Christ. She must be aware that she takes a great risk, because her authority is a subject-authority, itself under the judgement and correction of God. The Risen Christ, like the widow, keeps bothering her (Luke 18:5). Her availability, as a late comer, is already a grace, allowing the Lord to transform and to use her: "I have pleaded with the Lord three times for it to leave me but He said 'My grace is enough for you: My power is at its best in weakness'. So I shall be very happy to make my weaknesses my special boast so that the power of Christ may stay over me, and that is why I am quite content with my weaknesses, and with insults, hardships, persecutions and the agonies I go through for Christ's sake. For it is when I am weak that I am strong" (2 Cor 12:8-10).

Fr Ion Bria
Professor of Orthodox Theology
Former Director of the Unit 1
Unity of Renewal of the World Council of Churches,
Geneva

WISDOM UNDERSTOOD BY MEANS OF THE SPIRIT
(FIDELITY)

September 12, 1987

Fidelity always finds a way to be with Me. Love Me and be faithful, child. Unseen are My Works from the wise eyes; I have them hidden from them. My hidden Wisdom I give to humble and to mere children.

Daughter, I am Spirit, and I have approached you, teaching you as Spirit to spirit. My Teachings were given to you spiritually and not in the way philosophy is taught. Vassula, be aware of what has to come, for an unspiritual person will not accept these works as from the Spirit of God; he will defy them because they are beyond his understanding, as these can only be understood by means of the Spirit. I, the Lord, know what the wise think, and I tell you truly, they do not convince Me.

MY FIRE
(PURIFICATION - THE NEW JERUSALEM)

August 17th, 1988

Lord?

I Am. I am your Redeemer - so trust Me. I have come, through you, to give My Message of universal Peace and Love and show to all My creation My Sacred Heart and how I love you. My Mercy is Great upon all of you!

Dearest souls, the time for your purification is drawing

near - what I will do is out of love; your purification will be to save you from the gates of hell. I will descend upon you like Lightning and renew you with My Fire. My Spirit of Love will redeem you by drawing you into Love to consume you into a living flame of love. I will let My Spirit pour out of heaven and purify your blemished souls into holy spotless souls - purifying you as gold is purified in fire. You will recognize the Time of Salvation, and when My Spirit of Love will descend. Unless this happens, you will not see the New Heavens nor the New Earth I foretold you.

My child, by My Fire, by My Love, by My Mercy and by My Justice, My seeds[1] will sprout and open like new lilies which face the sun - seeking My Light and My Dew; and I will pour from My Heavens, My Light, embellishing you and My Dew nourishing you to see a new era of Love. By My Power, I will sweep away all iniquity, perversion and evil; I will descend upon you like a violent torrent of cleansing waters and wash away all your evil and leave you standing upright as columns of pure gold. With My Torrents of Fervent Love, I will sweep away all that is false and faked(up) - just like clay is washed away with a few drops of rain, so will My Spirit of Sublime Love wash away your sins which blemished your soul.

I, your Saviour, will renew you creation and offer you **My Gift**. My Gift will descend from Heaven[2]. **A Glittering New Jerusalem; A Renovated Church - Pure and Holy**; because I, who was, is, and is to come, will be living in Her midst and in Her very Soul. You will all feel Her, palpating and

---

[1]Seeds : us.
[2]The Lord gave me an intellectual vision of millions of angels descending from heaven and holding a new city, like on a platter. A New Blessed Church was descending from heaven.

alive, because My Sacred Heart will be throbbing within Her. I, the Lord of Lords, am like on fire[1], and My Sacred Heart is in ardent Flames - so eager with desire to enwrap you all - thrusting you in My Furnace of Love and leaving you ablaze in total rapture and ecstasy of love for Me, your Beloved God! Yes, I will make out of each one of you a living altar, ablaze with My Fire.

O creation! When My Fire will enkindle your hearts you will finally cry out to Me: "You are the-One-God-and-Only, the Just One - you are indeed the Lamb. You **are** our Heavenly Father - how could we have been so blind? O Holy of Holies, be-in-us, **live-in-us**. Come, O Saviour!" and to this cry of yours, I will not hesitate. I **will** descend upon you, as quick as lightening, and live among you; and you, beloved ones, will realize that **from The Beginning** you were My own and **My seed**. I will then be among you and will reign over you with an everlasting love. I will be your God and you, My own.

Dearest soul, treat Me as your King - crown Me with your love.

DO NOT SUPPRESS MY SPIRIT,

September 15th, 1988
Holy Mother of Sorrows

Lord?

I Am.

---

[1]The Lord seemed very impatient, as 'on fire.'

*How is it that so many ministers do not appreciate Your Merciful Signs You are giving us these days? Lord, do You know what they are saying? They say that this is not Real Faith, in other words, "**we** are already converted without signs, so **we** can do without them, so God, do not give us anymore, **we** are not interested in such extraordinary things." Instead of them falling FLAT with their face to the ground and cry out to You, "Glory be to God! Praised be the Lord! for Your Boundless Mercy! You are indeed fulfilling the Scriptures! "What is Real Faith to them if they push away the Spirit? They argue by saying, 'remember what Jesus said to Thomas, "Happy are those who have not seen but still believe..."' have they forgotten what Scripture also says, "**Never** try to suppress the Spirit, or treat the Gift of Prophecy with contempt." And the Spirit blows where It wills... - When these people argue they do not seem to realize that they are only arguing with You My Lord.*

My child, cry out loudly to the nations - shout! so that everyone may hear, **"here is your God!** Our God is with us, He has never abandoned us, He has come like a Shepherd to feed His flock and gather His lambs in His arms - for His Kingdom is at hand." My little flock I shall feed and gather with great love all of them, in My arms.

They do not care for Your Signs, they hear of them and file them away. They seem to want to tell You to stop Your Signs.

Nobody needs to advise Me. I need not one of these counsellors, for their wisdom is shame to Me. Do I not know how to measure you and know how to feed you? Alas! Only a remnant of you is left who welcome My Spirit. Have they understood how, by having an antagonistic spirit, **they have failed Me**? And by having failed Me - failed to see The Truth? Does the clay say to its fashioner, 'what are you making?' **Receive humbly** what you get from the Spirit, accepting My Works and It's mysteries. I willed to augment My Signs in your days, so receive with joy what you get from the Spirit; rejoice and receive Me; be glad instead of turning your backs to Me; face Me and recognize Me! Do not suppress My Spirit - welcome Me instead! Alas for you who suppress My Spirit; alas for you blind guides - bloated with Vanity - you have made a desolation out of My Holy Church! Seek The Truth by examining yourselves to make sure that **you** are in **The Real Faith**!

Altar! I, the Lord, will keep your flame ablaze until the end. My Works are not yet finished. Come now. We? us?

Forever, amen.

HOW TO UNDERSTAND THE SPIRIT

September 25th, 1988

My God, having given a few of Your Messages to L... he said that they are embarassing to read, he felt uneasy reading them because of the Love You have for me Your creature and the love I have for You my God! He said, they are shocking. Lord?

I Am. I am God. I am Love. Whosoever says that My Messages are ignominious, is only condemning Me and by condemning Me is condemning himself. An unspiritual man has not the capacity to understand the Spirit by means of his mind, nor penetrate into Wisdom to be able to understand the Spirit. One has to open his heart and allow the Spirit to enter and thus meet with his spirit: and Wisdom will illumine him to see what the Spirit is; how the Spirit works; what the Spirit feels. I am God. I am the Source of Love, who created all of you out of My Boundless Love **to love Me.**

Praised be our Lord!

READ HOW MY SPIRIT WORKS - 1 Cor. 12:1-11
(MY CUP OF JUSTICE IS BRIMMING OVER)

October 11th, 1988

I have, since the beginning of this revelation, been telling you that My Church is in ruin and in this ruin vipers have nestled inside It and made their homes within Its depths. Ah Vassula!![1] How I suffer... I will have to come and untangle those snakes which are creeping all over My Holiest of Sacraments and throw them out of My Church all over again... My child, to live and be surrounded by this devastating wilderness **is** difficult and terrifying **but I am near all those who love Me and worship My Holy Name with love.**

I want to remind all those who tread upon My Heavenly Works that I am Infinite Wealth. Whenever I saw My creation fall into rebellion I always sent messengers, carrying My Word - for Rebellion turns the land you are

---

[1] God, with a loud cry full of suffering and pain, called out.

living in into deserts.   Although your ancestors rebelled, their doubts were never severe as your generation's, doubting that I speak to My chosen angels, giving them My Messages.   Today, My child, I have ministers in My Church who claim to believe in Me but refuse all My Divine Works I am offering you in your days and that come from the Holy Spirit!   Their aridity is condemning them and in the Day of Judgment I will judge them severely!   These peoples should go back to Scriptures and read how My Spirit works and how I bless the gifts I am giving to the chosen ones - they all come from Me[1].

My child, you and I, I and you, are crossing this wilderness - this deadly wilderness caused by Rationalism, lack of Faith, lack of Love, promiscuity, self-indulgences, vanity and a **resentment** to all that descends from the Holy Spirit. Their obduracy to listen is condemning them - anyone who rejects the Works of My Holy Spirit is rejecting Me **for the Holy Spirit and I are One and the same!...**[2] These people are promoting this desert and are making sure that **nothing** will grow in it; if they see a flower, either they will trample on it and crush it, or will ignore it on purpose and never water it so that it withers and in this way get rid of it... My Cup of Justice is brimming over and already they are sensing the first drops of My Justice upon them.   **All** I ask from these peoples, especially those who serve Me yet refuse the Holy Spirit's Works, is to **pray, pray, pray for enlightenment and for a stronger faith.**

Come, My child, please Me always by remembering My Holy Presence.

---

[1] Jesus asked me to mark I Corinthians, 12:1-11.
[2] Same essence, substance.

I AM THE SPIRIT OF LOVE

October 13th, 1988

My God?

I Am. I have loved you from all eternity and from all eternity I wished you to love Me. I am the Spirit of Love. Leave your soul open to Me so that My Love will reflect in you; be like a mirror opposite Me - I wish to reflect My Love in you. I, My Vassula, am not a harsh God; I am Gentle, loving even all those who despise Me. Flower of Mine, since you start to understand how much love I have for you, can you then understand how Love suffers because of this lack of love?

Yes Lord, I start to understand.

Then come to Me and console Me - do not deprive Me. You **can** console Me. Be blessed.

- THE ADVOCATE -
(I, THE LORD, DESIRE THIS UNITY)

December 20th, 1988

I have said to you all that the Advocate, the Holy Spirit, whom the Father will send in My Name, will teach you everything and **remind** you of all I have said to you. I am not giving you any new doctrine, I am only reminding you of The Truth and leading those who wandered astray back to the complete Truth. **I, the Lord, will keep stirring you**

up with Reminders and My Holy Spirit, the Advocate, will always be among you as the **Reminder of My Word.** So do not be astonished when My Holy Spirit speaks to you - these reminders are given by My Grace to convert you and to remind you of My Ways.

THE DOVE
(I WILL FEED YOU BEFORE THE VERY EYES OF YOUR PERSECUTORS)

January 29th 1989

I saw last night a symbolic dream. I entered a church full of people, Mass was still on, it was crowded and people were standing too, the air was full of incense. The priest brought a box with him and we all knew that inside this box was the Dove. Alive. He was to free it, so that it may fly around us, giving us joy. The Dove was liberated, flying around us; we all stretched our hands so that it may come upon us, knowing that if it did, it would be a Grace. The Dove which was of sky-blue colour, came towards me, I felt that I loved It and I knew too that It loved me. On my stretched arms towards It, It posed and sat on the tips of my fingers. There was around me an awesome joy, some people were surprised, some also hoped It came to them too. But It flew around again not stoppng, then once more It posed on my fingers; I took it in my hands carefully and pressed It lovingly on my left cheek near my ear, hearing the quick heart-beats It had, Its heart was throbbing - then I found myself alone on a road, a path, walking. On the side of this path, all along, unknown little animals were swallowing each other without mercy. On my way, coming towards me, to frighten me, was a rat holding still an animal in its mouth. I did not fear, and to show the rat that I was "master" I hastened my step. It realised this and so went aside, by the path, attacking a squirrel from behind, and literally swallowed it. Then, like 7m in front of me, blocking my way, and stretched from one side of the path to the other, was a snake. I thanked God for letting me see it, because it was transparent like cellophane, so that people do not see it and step on it, so that they are bitten. I did not fear it since I made up my mind to go over it, avoiding it. Suddenly, from behind me, on my right, another snake came, but it was different, because it was an "attacking" snake. It was also transparent with only a small design on its back. That snake was as thin as my fingers but as long as 3m. - I found myself trapped but immediately I was levitated from the ground, by my Heavenly Father, I was levitated like 3m above ground, still, I was afraid that this long smake might stand up and reach me, so My Heavenly Father floated me forward, passing above all these snakes and placed me on the ground near a friend. Both of us were standing at the end of the path; there was a wall, a dead-end wall. I turned my head to my right because I heard something. I saw the first snake, looking for something. I told my friend, who had not seen the snake: "Don't move, stay still" avoiding to say there was a snake, less out of fear, this friend would move. I saw the second snake come too, near the other one, then the first snake, hungry attacked the thin one with such ferocity, swallowing it up with an ugly noise. I felt relieved and in peace, knowing that that snake now is only interested to sleep and thus leave us alone in peace.

I will feed you before the very eyes of your persecutors. I will raise you to Me, less they tread upon you. I, it is who will pour My Dew of Righteousness upon you and **no man** will I leave to extirpate you flower! You are guarded by Me and in your own Abba's arms you are hidden. Have no fear - I am near. Love loves you.

MY SPIRIT OF GRACE
(LOVE IS THE ROOT OF THE TREE OF LIFE
SCRIPTURES ARE BEING FULFILLED)

May 1st, 1989

Peace be with you all. I am the Lord, Emmanuel, the Holy of Holies who manifests Myself through this weak instrument. I come to you little ones, a nation so highly favoured, to you I come exposing My Sacred Heart before your very eyes. My Sacred Heart is Holy, Pure and filled with Love, so awake as in the past. Awake from your lethargy, awake and feel Me. My Spirit is constantly poured out ever so generously among you, yet so many of you have still not understood... I, the Lord, have formed prophets ever since I have created you but My Own repeat what they have always repeated... they are still persecuting all My prophets, hounding them from town to town. Abel's Holy Blood is being shed without cease. These people ask Me for laws that are just, they long for Me to be near them but when I send them My Holy Spirit of Grace, they close their eyes and refuse to hear and allow their hearts to turn into granite; they gather together, chasing away My Holy Spirit of Grace as one chases away an evil bird. My Sacred Heart is in pain... **Open up! Open up!**[1] Do not block My Way! Remove those blocks that only hinder My people, whom you have starved, from reaching Me. I have come to **you**, to heal **you** and console **you**; I have come to bring you Peace and Love; I have come to fertilize My land and cultivate it's soil. **My Name is Holy** and holy are My precepts and My laws. Yes, I will water this thirsty soil with My Love and **I, the Lord, will keep pouring out My Spirit upon My**

---

[1] Jesus was crying out loudly.

children, blessing them.

Have you not noticed? Have you not noticed that I am preparing you to receive a New Heaven and a New Earth I had promised you long ago? Have you not **yet** understood? Have you not seen how I work? I beckon all of you from one corner of this earth to the other to **listen to My Voice.** Ah beloved ones, I have come to heal your sores, your wounds and your infirmities, which were all so savagely inflicted upon you in this darkness. No, beloved ones, your sores are not past healing, your injuries **are** curable for I-Am-With-You and ever so near you. **So come to Me with love, ask Me with love and you will receive, invoke Me with love and I shall hear you.** I will rise you to My Bosom and cradle you, comforting you. Hear My Cry of Love and Peace, Love loves you.

Love is the Root of the Tree of Life so let it be LOVE that comes out of your heart. When Love manifests Itself where there is evil, Love effaces all wickedness, dissolving it like mist is dissolved with the first warm rays of the sun. For the sake of My devout ones I will revive all corpses, I will not keep quiet; I will raise you all with My Word; I shall not be silent until I will Glorify My Body and renew My entire Church. Learn, all you who want to suppress My Spirit of Grace and who want to muffle down My Voice, that your evil efforts and your evil intentions are all in vain. I will keep stretching My Hand to everyone, even to the rebels, even to those who provoke Me night and day - see? You are all My people, no matter what creed or race. Remember, I am LOVE and I have created you all.

Today My Salvation Plan covers the entire world. I have been, and I am, sending you messengers in every nation to progress you in your faith, to convert you, to establish peace and love, to unite you, so do not try to muffle down

My Voice and My Mother's calls - Our Voices will keep coming upon you like a hammer shattering the rocks[1] until the Day of My Glory.

Rejoice and acclaim My Fruitful Vineyard, for it is by My Own Hand the soil is overturned and toiled; by My Own Hand the thorns and briars pulled out and burnt; with My Own Cape I shelter It from the dry winds and storms that arise from My enemy. I am Its Devout Keeper who fervently and forever watch over It. This vineyard is My Gift to you and Its Grapes will be offered freely to you and fill the whole world, feeding it.

Ah, My beloved of My Soul, listen closely to My Words and try and understand them - do not doubt, testing Me without ceasing... I, the Lord, am telling you most solemnly: **Scriptures are being fulfilled.** So why are so many of you surprised at the outpouring of My Spirit? Why are you surprised when your young ones see visions?

I come before you to revise your knowledge of My Word; I come with great love to revive the corpses of My sons and daughters; I come to convert you and remind you of My statutes; I come to call the sinner to confession; I come to call to repentance all those priests, bishops and cardinals who have so wickedly wounded My Sacred Heart and betrayed Me their Friend and God. I do not come as a Judge, not yet, I come to you as **The Beggar** in rags and barefoot with parched lips, imploring and lamenting for some love, for a return of love. Today you have in your sight a Lamenting Beggar with His Hand constantly outstretched, begging you for a return of love. **"I beg you, come back to Me and love Me; learn to love**

---

[1]Rocks = hearts out of stone.

**Me, learn to love Me; make peace with Me, make peace
with Me - I will not reject you. I Am Love and I love you
everlastingly."** Come to Me when the Hour has not yet
come - do not wait for My Justice to arrive, do not let My
Justice take you by surprise and unaware.   Remember
then that I shall be in this terrible, awesome Hour, standing
before you as a Majestic Severe Judge and My Voice
which was that of a lamenting beggar shall turn into a
glare of a Devouring Fire, in cloudburst, downpour,
hailstones. My Breath will be like a stream of brimstone
which will set fire everywhere, to purify you and renovate
you all, uniting you into **One Holy People.**

Happy are all those who hope in Me and who welcome My
Spirit of Grace I outpour so generously now on all
mankind, for you shall see Me your God. Blessed are the
poor in spirit for theirs is the kingdom of heaven; happy
are all those who have ears to hear and are simple at
heart, welcoming My Spirit of Grace with a child-like-faith,
for in these little hearts My Word shall take root. Blessed
are those who are persecuted in the cause of right for
theirs is the kingdom of heaven.   In just a little while, My
little doves, and I shall be with you - have My Peace. I
bless each one of you. I, Jesus Christ, bless and forgive
your persecutors, for they know not what they are doing.
I, the Lord, love you all eternally.

ST MICHAEL

July 4th, 1989

I am Saint Michael. I am your Saint Michael to whom you
pray for protection and for defending you against the evil
one. Have no fear, your hardships will be redressed by

this prayer.

Allow the Spirit of Love to expand His calls of Grace, listen to the Spirit of Grace, listen to the Spirit for His Mercy is Great; do not suffocate those who receive the Holy One's Messages like your ancestors by saying to the seers "see no visions" and to the prophets "do not prophecy to us for **we** are in the Truth." Instead, lift up your eyes and look around - all are assembling and coming back to God, your sons from far away and your daughters being tenderly carried, for the Lord has announced this:

> **"Though night dominates your era, My Light shall pierce it and will cover this earth and all nations shall come to Me and My flock I will gather again into one Holy Fold under My Holy Name."**

Pray, O children of the Lord, and allow the Lord to redress His people by accepting what comes out of the babe's mouth and the lowly. Have no fear, salvation is near and at your very gates. I bless you in the Name of the Father and of the Son and of the Holy Spirit. Amen.

DISCERN WHAT COMES FROM THE SPIRIT
(LACK OF DISCERNMENT PRODUCES UNRIPE FRUITS)

July 28th, 1989 - Rhodos

Be one with Me. How I the Lord love you! See? My Sacred Heart is open and he who wants to step in It is welcome. You are all free to choose, if you choose My Sacred Heart, I will fill you, I will let you live in My Light, you will absorb from Me. I will nourish you, then I shall ask you if you are willing to share with Me. Like a Spouse and a Bride we will share and I shall renovate you entirely with My Love.

Lord, make everyone come back to You. Renew our generation as in times past.

Come then, come back to Me. I am not rejecting you, I am all Merciful and ever so Compassionate. Acknowledge your sins, repent and be Mine. I-Am-He-Who-Saves; I am your Redeemer; I am the Holy Trinity, all in One; I am the Spirit of Grace and although your generation calls herself fatherless I am ready to forgive and forget and take back all those who have apostatised. My Holy Spirit of Grace is ready to lift and renew you. Why continue to reduce your lands into deserts? Are you not weary in having to live in wilderness? Return to Me, be one of those who have sought My Wells and have found them. I shall renew you with My Perfection, with My Beauty, with My Glory. I mean to raise you in perfection so that your soul may live.

I wish to speak to My beloved children[1] - I love them and My Love for them is eternal. I have called to show them My Heart and they have heard Me, they heard My cry from My Cross. I always desired to seduce their soul since they are My offspring. I desired this closeness to Me since the beginning of times and from all eternity I wished them to love Me and adore Me, their God. Come, I wish to remind them how I can manifest Myself in different ways and in devout souls, revealing My secrets, revealing My Wisdom. I wish them to learn how to discern what comes from the Spirit and what comes from their subjectivity. Since the beginning I have never ceased

---

[1] The group of Athens.

advising them to watch My Lips; lack of discernment produces unripe fruits, folly, presumption - it can only aggravate their hearts. I have raised them from their lethargy so that they may live and I had waited for this Hour ever so impatiently. With Me they will learn. Understand how My Spirit works.

I love you all and I do not wish you to fall into folly,[1] I do not wish you to be misled by your own subjectivity. Be humble, stay small and allow **Me** to feed you in the way I have chosen. I shall never cease watching over you. I, the Lord, give you My Blessings, My Love and My Peace.

THE EFFUSION OF MY HOLY SPIRIT
(A SMILE AT MY HOLY FACE AND I SHALL FORGIVE AND FORGET)

August 29th, 1989

Make my heart ready Lord to hear Your Word. I pray to You, Lord of Love, Lord of Mercy. In Your great Love answer me. God, shine on me and revive me with Your Light! Amen.

I am the Lord of the Harvest and since you have asked for labourers to reap this rich Harvest, I shall send you those helpers. Come nearer to Me now, approach. I[2] Am The Resurrection and The Life and I promise you that the Day of Devotion is not far now. Your dead will come to life again and all who still lie underground and buried by their sins, I will raise to life again. I will enlarge My Kingdom

---

[1] Some were claiming to 'hear' Jesus, and angels, whereas everything came from their subjectivity.
[2] Message for the prayer meeting.

and I will restore your lands which lie now barren and deplorable to look at. I shall repeat those Words from Scriptures: "does a woman forget her baby at the breast, or fail to cherish the son of her womb? Yet even if these forget, I will never forget you[1]."

I am preparing you a New Heaven and a New Earth and Love shall return to you and live among your remnant as love; and all these corpses you meet at each street-corner, I shall resurrect and like the wind I shall blow your shepherds back to New Pastures and with their shepherd's crook they will lead My flock to pasture as in the days of old. For even though their wickedness entered into My Own House and have deceived many and even though their sins made godlessness spread throughout the land, I am ready to forgive and forget and My anger would turn aside and would be as though it never existed, if even today they would recognize their fault.

But, still to this day, My Sacred Heart is broken from the lack of love and by the immense number of your era's sins, sins that have pierced My Heart and blushed Heaven; sins that defiled My Sanctuary and profaned My Holy Name. Yet, if you only knew how I am ready to forgive your era's crimes by just one kind look at Me - a moment's regret, a sigh of hesitation, a slight reconsideration, a smile at My Holy Face and I shall forgive and forget. I shall not even look at My Wounds. I will efface from My sight all your iniquities and sins, had you one mere moment of regret and all Heaven would celebrate at your gesture, for your smile and your kind look will be received like incense by Me, and that slight moment of regret will be heard like a new song by Me.

---

[1] Isaiah 49:15.

Today I descend upon you full of Mercy to redeem you for the sake of My Love. My Holy Spirit of Grace will be like mist and will cover this earth. I tell you most solemnly that I shall multiply My Graces upon you. My Word shall be revealed and heard by many and I shall multiply your visions. So all those who ignore My Holy Spirit of Grace and try to suppress It will be only kicking against a goad - all their efforts will be in vain, for I, the Lord, mean to resurrect you and cultivate this desert you are living in and make oasis out of your deceiving mirages.

I, your God, stand before you and ask those who still suppress My Holy Spirit this: "how is it that you cannot tell The Times? How is it that you have decided to leave My Signs and My Wonders unacknowledged? Why are you repeatedly muffling My Voice and repeatedly persecuting My prophets? Why are you fearing and ever so eager to extinguish the little flame you see that lights **your** darkness? Why do you rush to trample and annihilate every flower that grows with My Grace in **your** wilderness and aridity? How is it that you want Me, your God, silent and dead?" Let Me tell you then and remind you Who I Am,

I Am The Word and Alive
I shall Act.

While I was on earth, I had multiplied My bread and My fishes and fed multitudes, and when Moses crossed the desert with thousands and had nothing to eat, the stores of Heaven opened and fed them all with manna, and so it is today. Since the earth lies in desolation and cannot produce sufficient bread to feed you, I, with My Spirit of Grace, shall multiply My bread to nourish you, beloved ones, you who are starved and neglected. In your days, this is called, **"The effusion of My Holy Spirit."** You will be nourished directly by Me for I mean to keep multiplying My bread and leave no one hungry.   **Woe to those who try and prevent My children from coming to Me in these times of Grace!** So open your heart, you who still doubt, not your mind.

My teachings are sound and healing. Do not fear, believe in simplicity of heart. Do not judge and abuse My angels sent by Me with My Spirit - not even the Archangel Michael when he was engaged in argument with the devil about the corpse of Moses dared to denounce him in the language of abuse.   All he said was, "let the Lord correct you[1]."

Hope in Me, have Faith and Love Me. Live Holy for I am Holy.   Fast and amend.   Repent and offer Me your abandonment daily to Me; abandon yourselves into My Hands and I shall make out of you living columns of light. Pray without ceasing, pray with your heart. Receive Me[2] in purity and My Graces shall pour upon you.   Come at adoration time and adore Me. Confess your so many sins. Please Me, your God, and walk with Me.   Follow My precepts and do not look left or right, be perfect! **Be My Heaven!**

O creation, if you only knew how I your God love you, you would not hesitate to follow Me in My Footprints! Why look elsewhere for consolation? My Sacred Heart is the balm to your wounds, My Sacred Heart is **your** Home. My Eyes are upon you all. I bless each one of you, I bless your families, I bless all those who read this Message leaving My Sigh of Love upon your forehead. Love loves you all. Be one.

---

[1] Jude 9.
[2] Holy Eucharist.

FIRE OF LOVE

September 6th, 1989

Listen and hear: have you ever heard of anyone who tried to live in devotion to Me and was never attacked or persecuted?

No Lord, some of them even died as martyrs.

Yes, so you see little one we have now confirmation of what was said in the prophecies - to this day whoever comes forth from My Mouth and raises his voice to deliver My Message is sure to be persecuted by the Cains. I call them but they refuse to listen; I beckon, but no one takes notice. They are spurning all My warnings; they make fun of the promise. Have I not said that in your days I shall pour out My Spirit on mankind? And that I will put My Laws **directly** into your hearts and write them on your minds? **No prophecy** comes from man's initiative, how could it? My Word is given by My Holy Spirit, thus making men speak of Me.

I, the Lord, have promised you New Heavens and a New Earth and My Vassula, I am in full preparation of these! but people are self-centred in your days, irreligious, heartless, preferring their own pleasure to God; but the days are fleeing and soon all this wickedness will come to its end, swept away and cleaned by My **Fire of Love**. So courage little one, hardships there will always be, but My Strength will always sustain you. Soon you will see My New Heavens and will live on a New Earth, for My promise is soon to be fulfilled and a renewal of My Church is on its way. Already you are living in the beginning of its birth-pangs, so courage My beloved ones, you who bear My

Name and are My offspring - do not despair, My Word is being fulfilled.

I have said that I-shall-be-with-you and live among you - you shall eat directly from Me and I shall offer you water from the Well of Life free to anybody of you who is thirsty.   My Fire is already coming down on you from Heaven and consuming you with My Great Love; I will spread this consuming Fire from nation to nation, transfiguring your wickedness into love, enticing your petrified hearts leaving them ablaze, and your lethargy into zeal for Me your God. This Sacred Hour of My Fire will be spreading among you like a burning furnace and you will be filled with My Fire of Love, the Fire of My Holy Spirit, similar to the last Pentecost. I shall renew you, enlarging My Kingdom of Truth, Unity, Justice, Peace and Love, so rejoice! Exult with all your heart My beloved, I will come and remove all your proud boasters who were one of the reasons of your dispersion and your downfall. They who muffle down My Spirit, shall be overpowered by My Breath - you shall be purified by My **Fire of Love**.

Daughter, love Me, adore Me, please Me. Love loves you. I bless you My child.

ACCEPT MY HOLY SPIRIT OF TRUTH
(APOSTASY, THE FRUIT OF RATIONALISM)

September 13th, 1989

Lord, those who refuse all private revelations have as an argument that the only true revelation is the Holy Bible, this we all know, but what do You say my Lord?

The Holy Bible is indeed The Truth, the True Revelation, but I have not ceased to exist. Look, I am The Word and I am active in Spirit. My Advocate is with you all, the Spirit of Truth that many tend to forget or ignore, for all that the Spirit tells you is taken from what is Mine - He is the Reminder of My Word, the Inspiration of your mind. This is why My child, I am continually recalling you the same Truths. Understand the reasons and why I am constantly stirring you up with The Reminder. Accept My Holy Spirit of Truth. I come to remind you of My Word, I come to call you to repent before My Day comes.

Child, evangelize with love for love. Beside you I am, never fear. Ecclesia will revive, since Love is the Root of the Tree of Life and is among you. I shall feed this dying generation with the Fruit of My Tree, placing It directly into their mouths. Allow Me to use you as My tablet. Eat from Me. Come, we, us? Yes, I am together with your Mother. I love you, aghapa me[1]. Pray Vassula, please Me and come often to Me in between your daily work.

I often leave whatever I am doing at home to come and be with Our Lord even for two minutes, the nostalgia for God is such.

Delight Me and show Me that you are linked to Me. Remember the ransom that I paid for you, so come to Me anytime and talk to Me. Stay small. Understand how I, out of Love, will call every soul to Me. I want you to understand that the heart of your wise is in the house of mourning, they tend to forget in their so-called great stature My Power and My Divinity.

---

[1]Love Me in Greek.

Their corruptibility blinds them leaving in them an open space for Satan to speak to them, for they have shut their heart to Love; their mind and their heart are closer to the rational world than My Spiritual World. This plague has infiltrated into My Church; many of My shepherds are like those crows in the parable that I have given you - they are the cause of so much discordance in My Church. Their speeches and sermons lack Spirituality, faithfulness to My Word and My precepts; they repudiate My Mysteries in My Presence; they flout piety. Remember the deeds performed by their ancestor Cain? They have adopted his language, serving vice instead of virtue, immorality instead of purity. They have submitted without reservation to the slavery of sin - these Cains are alive to sin, but lifeless to My Spirit of Truth. When My Day comes they will have to answer Me and give Me accounts for not having guarded the Traditions of their Shepherd. Today, their mouth is condemning them and their own lips will bear witness against them - **it is the fruit of their apostasy.**

But Lord, listen to the cry of Abel, do not let us lie alone here with no one to lift us! Your House is in ruin, Your House is our Shelter, and we have nowhere else to go. Thousands will die from lack of bread, we are living among the rubbles. Hear our voice and Your children's laments, **hear Your Abel!**

My child! Be praying, never cease praying. Daughter, I promise you that I shall enter into My Temple unexpectedly and with a loud Cry I shall say to Jerusalem[1], **"be rebuilt!"** and of the Temple[2], **"let your foundations be laid"** and She will be My New City[3], alive

---

[1]That is: us.
[2]That is: our soul.
[3]That is: us.

with My Spirit, and Love shall dwell among you all My beloved remnant and I shall fill Her with My Trees of Life, and you, My beloved ones, will eat to satiety. I am the Light of the world and He who shines on you. Be alert and do not sleep for the days are counted.

Have My Peace My child. I, Jesus, love you - allow Me to feed you and this starving generation. Rest now in My Sacred Heart, I shall never fail you. Love is near you.

I COME AS THE REMINDER OF MY WORD
(THE DESIRE OF GOD)

October 2nd, 1989

Jesus?

I Am. Come, My child, take My Hand and we shall work together. I am Wisdom, your Teacher, so depend on Me only. Learn that no one is able to give you better knowledge than I, who Am the Lord. Listen and write:

Creation! Soul! You who read Me, you who hear Me, praise Me, glorify Me, praise Me from morning till night, praise and extol Me without ceasing; amend for those who never praise Me nor glorify Me; bless Me, worship Me and desire Me. Has no one told you of the Song of the Three Young Men?[1] Then learn and proclaim this among the nations, the Spirit of Truth is with you all.

My little children, I will remind you that I am God whom

---

[1] To be found in the book of Daniel 3:52-90.

you come to meet and pray. Since I am a living God, I feel if you come to Me with a lip prayer. I want you to desire Me, desire Me, desire Me; thirst for Me, seek Me eagerly. Have no other desire but Me; desire to be in constant link with Me; desire to please Me; desire to feel Me and hear Me; desire My Presence, let nothing of this world deceive you for if the world hates you, remember that it hated Me before you. **Place Me as First** - do not wound My Sacred Heart by neglecting Me. Near Me you will feel My Love, My Peace and this harmony of Heaven that I have with My Angels can be yours too if you come nearer to Me. I love you all with an eternal love, a love you are unable to understand on earth. Come and I shall show you, if you are willing, what **True Life in God means. I tell you solemnly that anyone who lives in Love lives in Me, your God, and I live in him.**

Wake up from your sleep, wake up from your lethargy and do not deceive yourselves saying, "but I love the Lord and He knows it, I always have and so my conscience is clean." Today I am telling you to return to Me. If you ask, "but how are we to return?" I will tell you, by converting yourselves, and if you say, "but we are converted, how are we to convert?" I will tell you then, by desiring Me, by thirsting for Me. Seek Me the Holy One; come and adore Me. Let your portion be Me, your Holy One. Let your eyes dissolve in tears of love in My Presence. Be alert, be alert - if you knew how much more alarming it is not to know the cause of your sins, not to feel your sins and to have lost the sense of what is good and what is evil! Resist the devil's tactics; be awake in your prayer; be in constant prayer to Me. Pray without ceasing. Let Me feel you are in a constant desire for Me, a constant prayer. A prayer coming from your heart is, **The Desire of God.**

My beloved ones, if you wish to grow in My Love do away

with your lethargy and your lip-prayers. **To be in constant prayer is to desire Me your Lord.** Try and understand My Message. Desire Me with joy; desire Me with your heart and not with your lip, let Me hear you cry out "**Abba!**" So come to Me as little children again, return to Me and **ask Me with your heart, seek Me with your heart.** Come to Me, offering Me your heart. Devotion will embellish your soul. Do not stray from the Truth, for the Truth is Love - so come to Me full of Love, drawing from My Heart. **Be in the Truth, live in the Truth by desiring Me without ceasing** - do all these things so that you may live.

In these last days I am outpouring My Spirit of Grace on all mankind. Have you not noticed that I give even to the least? My Spirit of Grace is being poured on your generation to teach you to love Me. I come as the Reminder of My Word; I come to brighten this darkness with My Light; I come to warn you and wake you up from your deep sleep. I do not come with wrath, I come with Love, Peace and Mercy to unveil the shroud of death enwraping your nations. I come to remind you that I am Holy and holy you should be living; I come to remind you and teach you how to pray. I have given you everything to rise your soul to Me and share My Kingdom. I am coming to you as a Beggar pleading you. I am coming to you as Wisdom, teaching you all over again the knowledge of Holiness, ever so ardently. I offer you My Heart. Ever so humbly I offer you Myself every single day as your daily Bread; I give you Food to eat to your heart's content, eating your fill. So come to Me, return to Me and praise Me your God. I bless you all, leaving My Sigh of Love on your forehead. Love loves you all. Be one.

LISTEN TO THE VOICE OF MY SPIRIT
(PRAY IN SILENCE)

October 10th, 1989

My soul yearns for You today. I have given You my heart and my soul to form. My Lord has come to me in all His splendour and majesty to lift my soul to Him to show me His Great Love and Mercy. He has lifted me with tenderness to acclaim to all nations His Infinite love and His Mercy. His Love is everlasting.

Beloved, stay small so that you may easily creep into My Sacred Heart. Love loves you. Listen and write:

Peace be with you all. I am Peace; I am Love; I come to your nation out of My Boundless Mercy to stretch My Vineyard in your land too, so that its Fields yield enough fruit to feed your dying nation. My Divine Works are spreading all over this earth and all are good since they supply every want in due time. Listen to My Voice devout children and blossom like the flowers blossom when spring comes; blossom with My Rays of Pure Light shed upon you. I am filling your nation's darkness with blessings; I want to heal your poor soul; I want to rest your weary soul - so thrust yourselves into My open Arms, I am your Saviour who calls you to **return to Me.**

You see My children, the spirit of lethargy has veiled many nations leaving many of them in deep sleep and I, from above, watch all this with agony and with pain. Today I, the Lord, am in search of your heart since what I need is love, a return of love. Come, come to Me with simplicity of heart, as a child approaching his father with confidence. Come to Me too, showing Me your weakness and telling

Me your problems, **let your Father in Heaven hear you.** I
am love, the Sublime Source of Love, who thirsts for a
return of Love, do not refuse My plea. Refuse the
temptations surrounding you, My child, refuse to give
Satan a foothold. If you only knew how near you I Am
and how eager I am to lift your soul to Me and wean you
to real Food! Try and understand Me, try and perceive My
Will, do not be here only to satisfy your curiosity, be here
to learn. Widen the space of your heart only for Me to
allow Me to make My Home in you.

Do not suffocate My Spirit in you with immorality,
rationalism, egoism and other sins; do not suffocate Me,
leave My Spirit to breathe in you and **lift your eyes to
Heaven and pray in silence as I have been praying to My
Father.** Pray with your heart and He will hear you; pray
with love and He will not refuse you; pray with faith and
He will not deny your plea. All that you do, do it with love
for Love and I will not remain silent or unmoved or
unresponsive to your plea, for I am full of Mercy and full
of Tenderness.

I am the Good Shepherd who seeks among the rubble My
lambs and My sheep. I come to seek you with My Heart
in My Hand to offer It to you; I come to seek you in your
poverty to remind you again that you are not fatherless
and that you all belong to Me; I come to remind you that
in My Father's House there **is** a room for you My child[1],
a room which belongs to **you.** My Soul is yearning for
you. My Soul is in unspeakable distress when every time
a room is left void for eternity. I, the Lord, bring to you

---

[1]Jesus said this very moved.

Heaven in My Hands[1] as a gift for you, to offer It to you but My enemy wants to prevent you from receiving It. So many times he is using poor souls to reduce My Voice into silence, rebuking the Graces of My Holy Spirit and thus injuring My Body beyond recognition. Hiding behind a Cloud of Darkness these souls become Masters of Evil and Vanity, refusing to grasp My Ways, these people weigh heavily in My Heart. Fearlessly they come to Me void and empty handed; they make fun of the Promise. They are once again placing in My right Hand a reed, jeering at Me, then remove it from My Hand to strike My Head with it; **then they go down on their knees to do Me homage** so that people outside the Church should speak well of them. Those sacrileges are re-crucifying Me every single day; they are dragging Me to Calvary repeatedly; they hate Me for no reason. Ah, My children... these people have turned My Eyes and the Eyes of My Mother into an eternal waterspring.

Listen to My Cry from My Cross, for innumerable multitudes are constantly falling into the eternal fires; listen to the Spirit that brings life. Your nations have grown coarse at heart and have forsaken the fountain of knowledge. Turn your eyes to Me! Lift your heads to Me! Come and absorb My Light; allow Me to remove your shroud, enwraping your nation.

I am the Guardian of your soul and of your heart who implore you for a return of love, a love without self-interest. Die to your own self and allow your heart to be directed by the Spirit and the Spirit will lead you to the Truth, acknowledging Me. Listen to My Voice, the Voice

---

[1] I saw in an interior vision Jesus holding in His Hands a most sparkling and luminous globe, reminding me of the luminosity of St Michael the Archangel.

of My Spirit. Augment your prayers and live holy - be holy
for I am Holy.

COME HOLY SPIRIT
THE THREE IRON BARS

October 26th, 1989

Vassula, draw three iron bars with a head on the top
- these represent the Roman Catholics, the Orthodox and
the Protestants. I want them to bend and unite but these
iron bars are still very stiff and cannot bend on their own,
so **I shall have to come to them with My Fire and with the
power of My Flame upon them they shall turn soft to bend
and mould into one solid iron bar, and My Glory will fill the
whole earth.** ΙΧθΥΣ ⊰⊱

Pray often to the Holy Spirit this prayer:

> Come Holy Spirit, come
> through the powerful
> intercession of the
> Immaculate Heart of
> Mary your Beloved Bride.
> Amen.[1]

With this prayer My Holy Spirit will hasten and come upon
you. Pray for the effusion of My Holy Spirit to come upon
you.

---

[1]Prayer shown to me.

THE POWER OF MY FLAME
(A HEAVENLY CHURCH)

November 2nd, 1989

The Lord is constantly these days showing me the "three iron bars." This time I see them a bright orangy colour, because they seem to be very hot.

My Vassula, with My Fire and with the power of My Flame, not only will I soften these iron bars, but with My Breath I shall melt them altogether and form them into one solid bar forever and ever - then you will all reach the fullest knowledge of My Will and My Understanding. This will be My Gift to you - a heavenly Church. It will be radiant with My Glory and your hymns shall be sung around one Single Tabernacle and your land of ghosts shall revive again, **transfigured and resurrected.**

Come daughter, Wisdom shall instruct you. **ΙΧΘΥΣ**
I bless you - love Me.

I AM AN ARDENT FLAME OF LOVE
(BE MY HEAVEN)

November 30th, 1989

I heard again the Holy Spirit praying for me without ceasing during the whole night and in the end, very early in the morning the Holy Spirit asked me to repeat after Him this prayer: "Pere aide moi, car Ta Puissance est Amour" it was given to me in French, and it means:

"Father help me, because Your Power is Love."

Lord, in spite that many nations have sunk into a pit of their own making, and caught by the feet in the snare they set themselves, have pity on them. Lord, grant them a hearing, make out of them a completely new batch of bread, glorifying You my King. I shall ask You again Lord of Love, Lord of Mercy that those who heard and heard again but never understood, to hear this time for the sake of Your Love and that those that saw and saw again but never perceived, to perceive this time, for the sake of Your Great Mercy, entering thus into Your Mystery. Soften their heart so that they may understand fully with their heart and not with their mind, and thus be converted and healed by Your Divinity; then they shall realize how wonderful Your decrees are, and their soul shall not resist but respect them.

My child, I shall glorify My Name again - just wait and see. This is only the beginning.

Lord, You are like a consuming Fire and I know You are working in many hearts. Lord I live for You, be very near me in this exile.

Saturated by Me - live for Me, live under My Wings. Imbued by My Love - flourish now and grow, spread your branches like a terebinth. Tell Me that I am He whom you love most; be My song little one; be My Heaven and glorify My Holy Name again. Lean on Me when you are weary, oh yes! Delight Me and feel My Presence! Oh yes! Hunger for Me, thirst for Me - look at your King! Behold the One who saved you! Look flower at My Beauty! **Free** My dove, free at long last. Enter now into My Sacred Heart and let It consume you entirely and make nothing else out of you but a living flame of Love's jealous Love.

I am an Ardent Flame of Love and My Love is indeed a consuming Fire. Desire Me. I am being glorified. Stretch this love for Me - My Hand is upon many nations. All shall be accomplished soon, on the right hour and the right time. Love Me, desire Me. Come, we, us?

Yes Lord, for eternity. Glory be to God.

MY HEAVENLY BREAD
(THEIR PRUDENCE BECOMES IMPRUDENCE)

December 6th, 1989

My Lord, teach me if it pleases You, to be patient, like Job was patient and clung on You.

Depend on Me, I shall teach you My own patience.

My Lord, if it is Your wish, infuse in me courage just like Your disciples.

My flower, I shall remind you how I endured My Cross disregarding the shamefulness of It, then you will not give up for want of courage. You are guided by My Spirit. My aim is to bring atheism at its end.   Ah, My child! Not many will listen to My Voice because your generation **lacks humility**; each time I approach My children through weak instruments, My own, many of My own muffle down My Voice; daughter, their prudence becomes imprudence since they do not recognize the fruits of My Divine Works and refuse to believe. But as I have said before, they do not believe because they are no sheep of Mine. The sheep that belong to Me listen to My Voice, I know them and they know Me and follow Me -so in their case these prophecies are being fulfilled: "at the end of time, there are going to be people who sneer at religion and follow nothing but their own desires for wickedness. These unspiritual and selfish people are nothing but mischief-makers"[1] and "you are reputed to be alive and yet are dead". "Wake up" I tell you, "revive what little you have left - it is dying fast."[2] Not only they are dead but in their fall want to deprive My children from eating My Heavenly Bread too -they are forgetting that I rule over them and that I confer My Spirit of Grace on whom I please and raise the lowest of mankind. In their wickedness they shut the door at My Face. Resentful to My angels, they abolish all hopes from this generation - they treat My Holy Spirit of Grace no less better than the Pharisees treated Me on earth.

My Vassula, beloved of My Soul, courage - let Me tell you this: I have placed you all[3] on My Path to share My Cross of Peace and Love.

TODAY, THE HOLY SPIRIT OF GRACE IS INDEED THE KEYSTONE

December 23rd, 1989

Peace be with you daughter, touch My Heart. Feel how lacerated My Heart is.

With my spirit I felt Our Lord's Heart.

---

[1] Jude 1:18-19.
[2] Revelation 3:2.
[3] All those who one way or another participate the diffusing of these messages.

Remove the thorns that now pierce My Heart.

Show me how to remove these thorns Lord.

Thorns can be removed by love. Love Me, love Me.
Vassula, be My balm; console Me and bring to Me small
souls - show them My Heart, tell them of My Love.
Remove each thorn and replace it with a small soul.
Tremendous reparations have to be done to My House but
I shall rebuild It, brick after brick, layer after layer. In spite
of the tremendous attacks My House receives, I the Lord
shall prevail in the end. I shall then fill up My House with
pure souls; like doves that fill up their cote so will it be too
in My Own House and I shall allow these pure souls to eat
directly from My Hand so that they learn to say, "Abba".
Divinity shall conquer corruption, corruption that through
the world's vices made out of My children atheists. I
intend to make out of these pure souls divine beings,
reflecting My Divinity - this is why I am in these days
reminding you without ceasing the Truth. Even though I
am repeating Myself, even when some of you get annoyed
because I repeat Myself, I shall continue to remind you of
the same truths - this is the only way to stir some of the
sluggish spirits.

Today My Holy Spirit of Grace is rejected by the
unbelievers, but they do not know what they are rejecting.
It is as Scripture says: "the stone rejected by the builders
has proved to be the keystone, a stone to stumble over, a
rock to bring men down[1]." These unbelievers stumble
over the corner stone because they do not believe in the
Works of My Holy Spirit. Yes, today My Holy Spirit of
Grace who descends to show you the Way, the Truth and

---

[1] 1 Peter 2:8.

the Life **is indeed the Keystone,** the Corner Stone that you do not recognize and reject altogether.

Daughter, even in your imperfection I shall be able to accomplish My Messages. Take your sufferings as blessings, think of what I had to suffer to accomplish My Work and through My Wounds healed you all. I, the Lord, need generous souls who are willing to immolate themselves for others and become little crucifixes - all these sacrifices shall not be in vain. Tremendous reparations have to be done and the time is pressing. So, little one, lean on My Shoulder when you are weary, do not fall. Lean on Me - united we are. Pray My Vassula for the cause of your era's salvation. Caress Me your God with your littleness, caress Me with your prayers coming out of your heart. **I want sincerity,** I do not want obligations. I want your heart. Be perfect! Come, My Eyes do not leave you, you are all[1] My Joy, My Happiness. *IXθYΣ* ✗◁▷

MY SPIRIT TEACHES YOU, REMINDS YOU, WARNS YOU
(THEY NO LONGER COUNT THE FRUITS OF OUR HEARTS)

January 10th, 1990

(To the prayer group of Switzerland).

Peace be with you. Feel My Presence. I am among you. Set your hearts to listen and understand My Words.

---

[1]Small souls.

Beloved children, it is now a little bit more than a year that I, the Lord, have been with you in this special way, giving you My Messages and in this way I have shown you the Wounds of My Sacred Heart. I have made known to you the state of My Church of today and the cause of the bitterness of My Soul. I have shared with you all My Cross of Peace and Love. I have made known to you My most intimate desires and my Holy Spirit has been reminding you of My precepts. I have been reminding you the teachings of My Church; I have assembled you because you are My Own and it is to My Own I come to show My Glory. I am in you and you are in Me. I am the Light of the world and you, My little ones, are the vessels carrying My Light and My Message of Peace and Love. I have assembled you as a shepherd gathers his sheep back in their sheepfold and have encircled you with My Arms, yet there are other sheep I have that I have to lead as well.

I am preparing you to live under the New Heavens and the New Earth because the time is drawing near now when Love is to return and live among you. Soon you shall be hearing Love's footsteps on the Path of return and it is for this reason all around the earth My Voice is heard, and it is for the same reason your young ones see visions. I have said that I will pour out My Spirit on all mankind and that your sons and daughters shall prophesy and that even to the least I will give My Blessings. Yes, My Voice today cries out in the wilderness. I am calling **each** one of you, yet some have failed to understand what My Spirit meant and have neither understood My Signs nor the visions of your young ones; they no longer count the fruits of Our Hearts but treat My chosen souls as imposters. I shall remain with you in this way for only a short time now, but I shall not leave you without making sure that you have shelter and pasture. I am your Good Shepherd who cares for you. I am the Lord who, like a watchman, watches you from above - how could I resist and not descend and take any means to reach you when I hear your laments and your agony? How could I resist and not rush to you when I see so many of you heading into the eternal fires?

I am coming to you in this way not to condemn you, but to alert you. I come to save the world. I do not come to condemn the world but the world will misjudge the Times again, as they had misjudged the Times of My Coming as the Messiah and have not recognized Me but treated Me as they pleased, handing Me over to the pagans. The world again misjudged the Times of he who was put to straighten the path before Me, they did not recognize John the Baptist who came in all righteousness as Elijah, but treated **him** too as they pleased. And today, your generation shall misjudge the Times once more, **because these Times are not in their favour.**

I have said that in the last days to come I shall be sending you Moses and Elijah on earth, but your generation shall not recognize Them, they shall neither hear Them nor understand Them but they shall abuse Them, rejecting Them as they rejected John the Baptist and Me as the Messiah.

I have said that in the last days many false Christs shall arise and I have advised you to be alert for these false Christs who, in your days, are the false religions. I have given you My Word and I have warned you not to set off in pursuit after these sects. I have given Peter the charge of My Church and I have asked him to feed you, to look after you and to love you.[1] I tell you solemnly, before

---

[1] 1 Jn 21:15-17.

this generation has passed away **all that I have been telling you will have taken place,** so do not be deceived but resist to your opponents, resist to those who oppose Peter. I Myself shall give you an eloquence to recognize what the Spirit today is saying to the Churches, **so do not prepare your defence.**

The fig tree has ripened and My Kingdom is near you now.[1] Pray for those who do not understand - to believe is also a grace given by Me. I have chosen you and this is why you will be persecuted but do not let your hearts be troubled, love one another and do not judge. Let this love I have shown you be the **emblem** of My new disciples so that they may recognize that you come from My Fold and that you are children of God and in God.

My little children, love one another as I love you. Do not ask for signs, be content to what the Spirit is giving you now. I tell you solemnly that soon there will be One Single Fold which shall be led and guided by One Single Shepherd.

I am Spirit and I desire you to worship Me in spirit and truth and not by dead words, therefore learn to pray with your heart. Pray for the whole Church. Be the incense of My Church and by this I mean that you pray for all those who are proclaiming My Word, from the Vicar who is representing Me to the apostles and prophets of your days, from the sacerdotal souls and religious souls to the laymen, so that they may be ready to understand that all of you whom I mentioned are part of One Body, **My Body.** Yes, all of you make one body in Me.

---

[1] Jesus said these words very majestically and as though speaking to himself.

Pray for those who refuse to hear, to be ready instead of reluctant, to hear a sermon or a revelation inspired by the Spirit. Pray that they may understand how My Spirit works in different ways and how My Spirit teaches you, reminds you, warns you. Pray that they may let My Spirit speak out. I reveal nothing new. I have told you all this beforehand so that your faith may not be shaken when harder times shall come. Remember little ones that someone who has never had his trials, knows very little.

I, for My part, shall constantly keep watch over you but I desire that you too offer Me your full abandonment so that I mould you as I please. I want you to be like clay in the hands of a potter; I mean to mould you all back into My Divine Image; I intend to give you back the divinity you once had, but lost.

Flowers of Mine, I am He Who Loves you most. I bless you all, leaving on your foreheads the Sigh of My Love. Be one.

RECEIVE MY HOLY SPIRIT
(THEY LEFT ME MAIMED IN THEIR BATTLE)

April 12th, 1990

Peace be with you. I am the Resurrection, if anyone believes in Me even though he dies he will live. I am the Holy Spirit of Truth, I am the Reminder of My Word who comes to you and stirs you up from your deep sleep. It has been said that My Spirit of Grace shall be poured out lavishly on all mankind and that your sons and daughters shall prophesy - all that Scripture says is being fulfilled. I am preparing you from Heaven to acknowledge the Truth;

I am encouraging you by displaying portents in heaven and on earth; I am giving to the poor and the small visions; I am sending you My Mother to instruct you as a teacher in different nations; I am displaying My Infinite Mercy like a banner above your heads, generation, to educate you and bring you back to divinity. If you would listen to Me today I shall lift your soul and you will reach the place of rest.

Generation! You have been worshipping long enough unnamed idols, lifeless idols, inventions that harm you to death. You accorded divine honours to these, corrupting your life. For years I have not heard the sound of your voice, nor of your step, you have not invoked Me nor praised My marvels. Ah generation, why have you rejected Me your Holy One? Come and listen to Me again. Love will be coming back to you as Love, this is My Promise. So be prepared to receive Me and I shall give you the gift of My Love and the gift of My Holiness.

Beloved ones, you who are gathered here today, learn that it is I, Jesus, who sought you and called you all the way from the desert to enter My delightful Garden, **My Assembly.** I am the Sacred Heart ever so sensitive who asks you to make peace with Me and reconcile with Me. Let those thorns encircling My Sacred Heart bloom into a wreath of flowers. Open your heart to Me and welcome Me, offer Me your heart and I shall ravish you to delight My Heart. Speak to Me with your heart and I shall not remain unresponsive. Realize that I, who am your King and Sovereign of all, descend all the way to you in this world drenched with sin to seek you My friend, how much longer do I have to seek? My Eyes are worn out looking for your welcoming response to My Spirit of Grace. I open My Mouth, panting eagerly for your response, but the word is not even on your tongue. My Spirit of Grace cries out to you to lead you in the depths of My Sacred Heart, but today My Spirit of Grace gets no gratitude for His Mercy.

I bend all the way down to you from My Throne to your door. I come to you weary and as a Beggar in rags, wounded beyond recognition, barefoot and forlorn. Hear My laments, it is I the Christ. I am thirsty. I am thirsty for lack of love; My Lips are parched for thirst of love; My Mouth dryer than parchment from repeating My pleas; My Heart is sick with love. I love you to distraction in spite of your awesome pride and wickedness. I come to **you** My little ones with My Heart in My Hand, I know how poor you are but can I share your meal with you? Will you quench My thirst? Will you appease My Wounds? No, you have not sought Me, it is I who sought you and found you naked in this desert you are living in. Allow Me to enter your heart and I shall adorn you majestically. If you allow Me to enter your heart, I shall make you see My Wounds given to Me in the house of My best friends, you shall be awed by their depth and struck by the numerous marks savagely inflicted on My Body. **The Wounds of My Body are such that they left Me maimed in their battle.**

I tell you solemnly, anyone who does not welcome the Kingdom of God like a little child will never enter it. Seek Me in simplicity of heart and you shall find Me. Do not put Me to the test and **you will see Me**, recognizing My Omnipotency; do not stay aloof and cold to Our Calls; do not be deaf to Our Calls, hear Our supplications, open your ears and recognize the Shepherd's Call. If you are weak I shall lift you and I shall carry you on My Shoulders. I am ready to blot out every sin of yours in My Purity and My Light.

O friend! Why do you still waver with hesitation? Your navel-string is still attached to Me. I am the Source of your breath, I am the Bountiful all-nourishing Source and it is with My Word that I give you life and preserve you from death. It is not the various crops you eat My friends that give you life, it is I who give you life. Lift then your eyes to Me and treasure My Word in your heart and you **shall** live! Come and ask Me to open your eyes and I shall come eagerly and pull away your veil My friend; come and ask Me to bring you back from your exile, where many of you strayed and I shall come flying to you. Even if you have built a wall across My Path in the time of your wickedness, to divorce Me from you, I shall with one blow of My Breath pull down that wall. Then I shall remind you of My Love, I shall remind you that I am He who loves you most and that your abode is My Sacred Heart; I shall remind you not to differentiate yourselves in Me; **I shall remind you to be united in heart and soul** and love one another as I love you.

Yes, it is I, the Constant Reminder of My Word who speaks to you to refreshen your memories. Receive My Holy Spirit. I bless each one of you and at this very instant I shall leave on your forehead the Sigh of My Love. Be one.

THE OUTPOURING OF THE SPIRIT

April 22nd, 1990

It was the stone rejected by the builders that proved to be the keystone, Psalm 118:22. My Lord Jesus, You were rejected then as the Messiah because their spirit was not prepared, their hearts were closed and hard, yet You proved to be The Keystone. In our generation my Lord,

*the effusion of Your Holy Spirit is also rejected by the
"builders" and yet one day Your Holy Spirit will prove to all
of us that He was the Keystone.   By denying and
suppressing Your Holy Spirit that comes to us as **the
Reminder**, "the builders" are preparing again their own
downfall.*

See how former predictions have come true?   Indeed, I
have said that the Advocate, the Holy Spirit, whom the
Father will send in My Name will teach you everything and
remind you of all I have said to you, but I knew all along
that only a remnant would listen and return to Me.   On
these very ones who would listen to Me I shall invest with
My Holy Spirit of Wisdom an Insight, yes, I shall invest
them with My Spirit of Counsel and Knowledge and the
flickering light that now is left in this world will become a
vivid fire.   I repeat that My Holy Spirit of Grace is being
sent out to the four corners of the earth to teach you to be
holy and raise you up again into divine beings.   The earth
shall turn into a copy of heaven and thus My Will will be
done, the prayer I have taught you to pray shall be
fulfilled.

*Lord! Turn then all of us away and quick from the path of
delusion.   May we be one, united and live holy as your
angels in heaven, like all souls who live in heaven and
undivided in Your Love, may we too share like them Your
Love in unity, so that the earth becomes a reflection of
heaven.   Let Your Kingdom come and renew the earth
with fresh things, let Your Holy Spirit in this second
Pentecost come quick to renew us with a new spirit of
love and transfigure us all into divine beings! Maranatha!*

Peace be with you.   I tell you truly that the days are
coming when My Kingdom on earth shall be as it is in
Heaven.   You shall not remain divided for long now under

these skies, soon you shall all be one and Love will be dwelling among you, this is My Promise. But, My beloved ones, this renewal shall not come without tribulations, like any birth, this renewal will have its birth-pangs too, but the pains will also be quickly overtaken by joy.

I am pouring out My Spirit on you generation to water your desert and to make rivers out of your dry soil. Yes! I shall water your desert and turn it into a Garden, eventually you will see the force of My Words and the splendour of My Beauty. I intend to bring you all back to divinity one after the other. I am your Hope, I am your Refuge, I am your Consoler, Almighty I Am.

Recognize the Times, recognize the gentle Breath of My Holy Spirit of Grace upon you; I am blowing now on your nations, raising up with My Breath your dead, turning them into a reflection of My Image; I am raising new disciples every single day to glorify My Name again and evangelize with love for Love. I ask you then, My beloved ones, to pray daily for My Second Coming which is the second Pentecost. Pray for the conversion of souls that they may convert before My Coming.

Come to Me as you are and lean on Me, as John My beloved one leaned on Me; you too, place your head on My Bosom and listen to Love's Heartbeats - every heartbeat is a call for Love. All I ask from you is a return of love. Love Me, adore Me, rejoice Me your Lord. I bless you, leaving My Sigh of Love on your forehead. Be one.

WHERE THE SPIRIT OF THE LORD IS,
THERE IS FREEDOM
(YOU ARE MY ALTAR)

April 24th, 1990

I rely on Your Love. Let Your love rest on us, let it live in us as never before.

Beloved one, all that I have given you was to draw you closer to Me and adapt you to being with Me. I have given you this grace because it pleases Me - I wanted to comfort you. This, My child, is for your salvation and I shall remain near you in this way till the end - you are My altar and I want My altar pure. I want to fill you with My ardent flame, My Fire, My Holy Spirit.

It was, daughter, only yesterday that I had found you caught and ensnared by the evil one, and today see? you are free. I, your Saviour, freed you and not only have I freed you, I have also given you Life. You were imprisoned and I have liberated you. You were naked but I have adorned you majestically. You were barren but I have prospered you and flourished you. Your knee had never bent to praise Me nor worship Me, your Lord, yet I bent all the way to you to reach you and anoint you, blessing you. I had never heard your voice acclaim Me nor had I seen you in My House coming consciously for Me, yet I came all the way to your house, in your room, to let you hear My Voice. I sang a song of Love to you, so that you in your turn go out to the nations and teach them My Song. I have dispelled your faults like a cloud, your sins like mist, rejoice then in My Presence soul! I shall continue to show to humanity My great Love and Mercy through you so that they may at last believe that it is I. **I am**

LOVE. This is how I shall summon My people and surround them with My Love. I shall be to them like a wall of Fire surrounding them and I will be their glory in their midst. Come, My Vassula.

O God, how I love You!

These words are like flashing jewels of a diadem. Yes, love Me your God, follow My first commandment without nevertheless neglecting the others. Rest now, without forgetting My Presence. We, us?

Yes my Lord, we, us, forever and ever.

I bless you, bless Me too.

I bless You my Lord and I thank You for all that You are giving me.

WISDOM IS GIVEN TO MERE CHILDREN
- MY FIRE SHALL PURIFY YOU ALL -

April 30th, 1990

Lord, my God, save us in Your Love. Raise us in Your Light and with Your Infinite Mercy forgive us. Make us strong in faith; unite us to be one so that we may say together, around one Holy Tabernacle, "there is one Lord, one faith, one baptism, and one God who is Father of all, over all, through all and within all."[1]

---

[1]Ref: Ephesians 4:5-6.

Try then to imitate Me.

Give us the wisdom then to imitate You.

Wisdom is given to mere children. Unless they seek Me in simplicity of heart, Wisdom shall not be given to them and as long as their intellect is at work, Wisdom will remain hidden and as a riddle to them.

Tear away Lord their intellect so that they may at last see with their eyes Your Beauty and Your Splendour!

Little heart, pray for them then, pray in these godless times, let your prayers be like blended incense. Pray that I may give them back their sight. Pray that I may go over to them and wake them up from their everlasting sleep. Pray My little one, you who had the Law brought to you by Me and directed by My Holy Spirit. Pray that they die to their sin and resurrect to Holiness, Love and Faith, and if there are any wise men let them show their wisdom by their simplicity of heart towards Me, their zeal to all that is holy and by their ardour to draw souls to Me -may all these things be done with humility and love. Remember that if you do not get what you ask it is because you do not pray hard enough and with your heart. Come now, never forget My Presence, I am your Holy One and the One who loves you most.

Lord, You are good, patient and forgiving, most loving to all who invoke You. Hear our prayers my Lord, although they may be of extreme poverty, have mercy upon us and open Your Ear. We are sinners and not saints, but You were known to go to the sick and heal them with Your Love. We are all sick, a sickly generation drenched in sin, come to us and heal us, helping us to believe in our unbelievable unbelief!

My Righteousness is eternal; My Love I have for you all is Infinite; My Compassion for the wretched and the sick is Great and beyond human understanding - ask and it shall be given to you. I open My Mouth panting eagerly for your prayers.

I ask and on behalf of my brothers too, that You come and save us Lord in Your Love. Return to us, purify us!

I shall return to you as Love and My Fire shall purify you all.

You have promised us a New Heaven and a New Earth Lord.

I have promised you more than that little one, I have promised you a new Jerusalem and I have promised you that I shall be living among you. I will make My Home among you, see? Very soon now I shall be with you.

Then hurry Lord, hurry, we are all waiting eagerly for the second Pentecost and the outpouring of Your Holy Spirit. The Second Coming.

Are you all prepared to receive Me? Why are you silent?

Because my Lord it is difficult to say these words, "many are not prepared to receive You."

Pray then for those who ignore Me, pray for the godless, pray for those who are not ready to receive Me, prepare yourselves! The fig tree is ripe and soon you shall be eating its fruit. Come, we, us?

Yes my Lord, we, us.

THE EARTH SHALL BE SET AFLAME
(PROPHECY)

August 4th, 1990

Rhodes

Flower, peace be with you. Fire, Justice, is soon to descend. Ecclesia shall revive. The earth shall be set aflame. *IXθYΣ* ᗧ⎯D

YOU PREACH AGAINST KILLING, YET YOU KILL MY SPIRIT
Taken from "The Ten Commandments" Message - Aug 5-29, 1990

August 5th-29th, 1990

And **you**[1], you who are reputed to be faithful to Me and hold firmly to My Name, I know all about you, yes, you are reputed to be alive and thriving and yet you are not, you are dead and decomposing. Repent! I had entrusted you with souls beyond number, but the devil traded with you to exchange them for his gold and silver. Yes, indeed! I know how you live now - you live like jackals[2] in hidden lairs[3], these lairs upon which I shall run an open

---

[1] Here Jesus calls out to the false prophet with a lamb's mask.
[2] The once faithful ones "sold" themselves to Satan and follow the beast.
[3] The lodges of freemasons.

highway[1]. I shall come suddenly upon you and expose your nakedness and when the Day comes I shall not allow you to eat from the Tree of Life. Listen carefully: you preach against killing, yet you kill My Spirit. You boast about the Law then disobey it because you have not understood the mystery of My hidden manna. No, you have not yet understood My miraculous feedings, nor the mystery of My Transfiguration.

I have promised you to keep you alive in the end of Times with My Celestial Manna. I said to My church in Pergammun:[2]

> "To those who prove victorious I will give
> the hidden manna and a white stone, a
> stone with a New Name written on it,
> known only to the man who receives it."

I am today offering you this manna reserved for **your** times, a Celestial food, a nourishment of My Spirit for your starved spirit. I pour out My Spirit in its fullness to fill up your interior desert and I am offering you My celestial manna free, **for this is the food of the poor...** But you have not understood, so you refuse to eat it and forbid others from eating it. I have already inscribed My New Name on the "white stone" which will be known **only to the poor.** You claim to be humble and poor yet you are neither humble nor poor. Your spirit is enthroned in the riches of Satan.

---

[1] That is: God will overthrow these lodges.
[2] Apocalypse 2:3,17.

THE WEDDING OF THE HOLY SPIRIT
(GOD WANTS EVERYONE TO BE SAVED)

September 25th, 1990

Our Holy Mother's Message to us all:

Peace be with you, beloved children. Allow Me to remind
you that the Lord knows each heart, the Lord is in search
of your heart. Come to Him with a pure heart and He shall
teach you - the Lord shall comfort your soul. He shall lead
you in His Path and in the Truth. I beg you, you who still
waver, do not shut your hearts to reason. Return to the
Lord and He will return to you. A Joy from Heaven will
now descend among you, a Light will shine in the midst of
you. Be prepared to receive this Light, be prepared to
meet the Lord.

Today, whose hands are clean? and who can say truly his
heart is pure? Whose soul is in perfect harmony with the
Lord? Beloved ones! My own! My children, the road to
the Lord is in the midst of you, **it is found in the land of
the living.** Stretch out then your hands towards His
Sanctuary and the Lord, from Heaven, will reach to pull
you to Him. Stretch out your hands towards Him and He,
full of Compassion, will lean down to you. Come to the
Lord without delay. Lift your eyes to Heaven and look to
no one else but Him, the Lord your God. Delight in no one
else but Him, your Saviour. Seek, seek no one else but
the Lord your Redeemer. Sing, sing to no one but to the
Holy One.

Am I to remind you that the Lord is Tenderness and
Compassion, slow to anger and rich in Graciousness?
Jesus was the Stone rejected by the builders that became

the keystone. I tell you truly that the Kingdom of God is among you and His Holy Spirit of Grace is blowing sweetly now on your nations to revive you, so come and see the Wedding of the Holy Spirit who will wed your lands. Do not reject the Holy Spirit that so manifestly is poured upon you, do not be like the "builders" who rejected the stone that turned to be the cornerstone. **God wants everyone to be saved.** And now this is My solemn warning to all who hear the prophecies of this book:

do not suppress the Spirit

the Spirit that now blows on you in the middle and in the peak of your apostasy. Do not say later on, on Judgement Day, "I had never heard, I had not known." Jesus and I are revealing things beforehand, before they happen, so that you cannot say when you meet God face to face, "I was unaware." The citadel of the proud shall fall and the devils shall be cast out from within her womb.

May you be blessed, may you all be blessed for hearing Me. I am your beloved Mother, the Theotokos who loves you all.

MY SPIRIT SHALL REST ON YOU
(MY MESSAGES ARE PRAYERS)

September 28th, 1990

Jesus?

I Am. Lean on Me. Lean on My Shoulder as I came to you and lifted you from the pit and carried you to My

House where I healed you - so will I continue to help your feet to be in the Righteous Path. Let your hands clutch on Me. I know you to be faint-hearted[1] but I shall make you strong to oppose evil.

Ah creation! **Mercy now descends before Judgement.** Welcome My Mercy **now** and My Spirit shall rest on you. Approach Me, you who desire Me, and take your fill from My Inexhaustible Wells of Life - for they who eat Me will hunger for more and they who drink Me will thirst for more[2], and I, like Manna, will replenish your soul and like a potter shall form you into what you have lost, **My Divinity.** Then I shall show you My Kingdom and I will send you Wisdom to teach you My Knowledge of My Holy things and I shall make you Mine forever and ever. You will be My sons and daughters glorifying Me together with My Assembly in Heaven. Then I shall send you out like mist to display like one displays a banner: **My Knowledge you received from Wisdom Herself** to teach others to grow upright in purpose and learning so that generation after generation My Holy Name may be kept Holy.

Your descendants would have a rich inheritance born of you and, thanks to My Infinite Mercy so will your children's children, and in the future the nations will know the meaning of **the Fear of the Lord.** My favours are not all past, My favours are inexhaustible, filling every valley, and My Tenderness is renewed **every day** upon you. I am pouring out continuously from My Heart My Love like flowing rivers to water your desert and revive you.

It is not I who forced you to dwell in darkness, it is not My wish to watch from above how you wall yourselves in and

---

[1]Jesus was smiling.
[2]Ecclesiasticus 24:21.

imprison your souls in the darkest dungeons. My desire is to bring you Home in peace; My desire is to make out of your deserts and parched lands, green pastures, to fill you.

Vassula, all My Messages are prayers. Read and write down Romans 8:26-27.

> *The Spirit too comes to help us in our weakness. For when we cannot choose words in order to pray properly, the Spirit himself expresses our plea in a way that could never be put to words, and God who knows everything in our hearts knows perfectly well what he means, and that the pleas of the saints expressed by the Spirit are according to the mind of God.*

Meditate upon this. I love you, repeat after Me this:

> Jesus, neither death, nor life, no angel, no prince, nothing that exists, nothing still to come[1], not any power or height or depth, nor any created thing, will ever come to separate me from You. I vow to remain faithful to You, this is my solemn vow. Help me keep this vow forever and ever. Amen.

---

[1]Romans 8:38-39

THE PARABLE OF THE WEDDING FEAST
I AM WHO I AM

October 20th, 1990

Jesus?

I Am. All I ask from you is love - this is My Theme. I need every drop of love in your heart. I want all the love you have to redeem those who are heading for the eternal fires. When I say, "revive My Church" or "embellish My Church", or "unite My Church", I mean you to pray, pray, pray without ceasing. Pray from your heart. Love Me fervently and with your expiations which will join these of My martyr saints, you will glorify Me. Yes daughter, with your expiations and your fervent prayers offered to Me with love you can alter coming disasters. You can alter natural disasters; you can extinguish the flaring wrath of My Father; you can relent Him, you can relent Him. You can embellish My Church; **you can bring together My People under My Name to celebrate mass around one altar;** you can repair their shepherd's staff, this staff they broke first in half then into splinters. For men this unity appears impossible, but for Me **everything** is possible. So pray and expiate for your brothers. I need victim souls, I need generous souls to repay evil with love, to repay evil with self-sacrifice. So offer Me your will and I shall make you My instruments of Peace and Love; I shall make you My instruments of Reconciliation and Unity.

*Lord, our own apostasies are rebuking us. Forgive us and help us to make reparations. Bring us back in the **love** of our bridal days, the early days, and remind us the affection we once had in our youth for You. Do not allow anymore any evil to overcome us.*

Yes, offer Me your prayers and I shall restore My House which is your House too. **Be loyal and this special favour will be granted to you.** Like in the transfiguration, I shall transfigure My Church to have all the radiant glory of Her youth, in Her bridal days. I will do all these things for the sake of My Holy Name. I shall unite you to demonstrate My Power.

Lord, there are other things too, I asked You this before but I would like to ask You again and I do not know how to say it!

I shall open your mouth and you shall speak![1]

Lord have You not said that the Advocate, the Holy Spirit, will teach us everything and remind us of all You have said to us? Then doesn't Scripture say... "in the Church God has given the first place to apostles, the second to prophets..".[2] and doesn't Scripture say... "there is a remnant, chosen by grace. By grace, you notice, nothing therefore to do with good deeds, or grace would not be grace at all!.."[3] and last doesn't Scripture say... "at all your meetings let everyone be ready with a psalm or a sermon, or a revelation..."[4] So why, Lord, nowadays most of the prophetic or private revelations are looked upon by some priests with contempt? With one eye instead of the two? and why are some priests and bishops even, attacking with contempt Your messages?

In reality, My child, they are wrestling against Me because they are suppressing the Advocate. Daughter, these

---

[1]Suddenly a flow of words came out of me.
[2]1 Corinthians 12:28.
[3]Romans 11:5-6.
[4]1 Corinthians 14:26.

people are not objecting to you. No, My angel, they are not, they are objecting to Me, not to you. If they ignore you My flower it is because you have grown in the middle of their desert - they will not water you so that you wither and fade away. They keep forgetting though that **I Am your Devout Keeper.**

Vassula, I shall remind you of the parable of the wedding feast.[1] Daughter, many are called but few are chosen. To believe is a grace given by Me, to have faith is also a grace given by Me. These are the Times of Grace and Mercy; these are the Times in which My Holy Spirit is poured out upon you; these are the Times when My Holy Spirit shall lift you out of your great apostasy, to wed you. Your era's wretchedness shall peel off your generation, because with My Own Hand I shall unwrap your death shroud to clothe you in the garments of your wedding.

Feel My delight My Vassula! Feel how I already rejoice at this coming event! My Holy Spirit will come to bring Fire to the earth, and how I wish it were blazing already! These are the Times of the Wedding of My Holy Spirit; these are the Times your King of Peace is sending His servants, His angels, His prophets and His Celestial Court to go out to the four corners of the earth and invite His friends to His Banquet and into His Kingdom and offer them His Celestial Manna. I have been sending My messengers in true righteousness all the way to your doorstep to announce My Return, but many of you did not believe them and treated them as imposters. Others would not come because they put honour from men before the honour that comes from Me. Since I have invited you and you have refused Me, since I have

---

[1]Matthew 22:1-14.

beckoned and you do not want to take notice, since you have ignored all My supplications and rejected Love's offer, I shall fill up My House and give My Kingdom to the rejects of your society to confuse you all. I shall give them back their sight and heal them, I shall open the Doors of My House wide open to let them in. My messengers will call aloud in the streets, and in the public squares. They will be sent by Me to invite the corpses they meet at each street corner, and those who have never been told about Me will see Me, and those who have never heard about Me will listen and understand. I shall be found by those who did not seek Me. Like I have revealed My Holy Face to you, daughter, I shall reveal Myself likewise to those who did not consult Me. Of My Spirit you do not want! neither of My Heart offered to you in My Hand! I tell you this now, before it happens, so that when it **does** happen you may believe that **I Am who I Am:**

My Kingdom will be taken away from you and it will be given to a people you call contemptible and foolish, the rejects of your society, and My House will be rebuilt and risen by those you call simple minds. They, with their love, shall restore the ruins of My House and all that has lain waste, and it is My Holy Spirit who shall shepherd them and console them... The citadel of the proud shall soon fall into a heap of dust. Justice shall prevail. Pray for these shepherds, pray for their conversion. Be blessed, My child. I shall not be long, soon you shall see Me face to face. I Am.

I HAVE GIVEN YOU SPIRIT-ANOINTED MESSAGES

November 23rd, 1990

Peace be with you. Daughter, do you wish to progress?

Yes Lord, I do.

Then My child, I shall help you progress, this is My wish too. Do not fall asleep, be awake of the dangers surrounding you. Flower, even though My enemies tear upon you and pluck out your petals, I shall always replace them - should they leave you crumpled up, do not fear. I shall pour from the heavens My Dew and revive you. Beautiful you should look and beautiful I shall make you and keep you - you are My envoy and you have nothing to fear of men.

If they accuse you because you call Me Father it is because they have not understood that the Spirit of Love you received and speaks through you, brings you peace and love to cry out, "Abba!" My Spirit is united to you My child. I have given you Spirit-anointed Messages for your era to revive you. Every word I have given you is Spirit and it is Life.

The sheep that belong to Me recognize My Voice from far. Soon I shall send My Light far and wide, from one horizon to the other. Yes, I shall make discipline shine out. Have My Peace, this is My Blessing. Love Me as I love you and remember, I am your King, so give your King the love He deserves! Be blessed. I Am.

THE HIDDEN TREASURE
(THE NEW HEAVENS AND THE NEW EARTH)

December 19th, 1990

Today I tell you, your Shepherd shall soon live among you and shall pasture His flock in the gardens of His City. No-o you are not yet one flock, but I shall fetch you one by one out of the desert. Therefore, My little flock, when from far you see your Shepherd coming up from the desert, know that I shall have with Me the rest of My lambs, and all the things I have done to you, daughter, I shall do to your brothers too. I shall save you. I shall unite you to your other brothers and Wisdom shall be your Holy Companion to instruct you without ceasing. I shall soon lift the ban and your great apostasy will come to its end and the prayer I have given you shall be accomplished. My Will shall be done on earth as it is in Heaven and under My Hallowed Name many nations shall come from far away, from all the ends of the earth, to dwell close to My Holy Name, extolling My greatness by the divinity I would give you back. And My Kingdom shall come because My Throne shall descend from above into My Holy City and I shall reign among the remnant left, who will see Me face to face. Love shall return as Love and My Will shall be done on earth as it is in Heaven because **you will be one**, worshipping Me around one Tabernacle with love in your heart and a Fire burning inside you. I shall accomplish My priestly prayer on earth as in Heaven. Your souls shall be rooted in Me, in Love, in Unity and filled up with the utter fullness of My Spirit. Yes, My beloved ones, I shall not only give you your daily bread but also a hidden Treasure out of My Heart - **The Celestial Manna**[1] that transfigures, uplifts your spirit into a copy of My Spirit. You shall be transfigured with the outpouring of My Spirit to know how to forgive fully those who trespassed against you. I shall put inside you a Spirit of Understanding and Mercy to make you understand what "the fear of the Lord means." Yes, beloved ones, and once you do, I shall give you Wisdom to be your travelling Companion and guide, to lead you into sanctity - this sanctity which will paralyse Satan, obstructing him from coming between us and between you and My Love.

So when you will see the sky dissolve into flames and the elements melt in the heat, know that this is the sign of the beginning of My Promise, and of the New Heavens and the New Earth, the Renewal of My Church, the Revival of My Church,

the Revival of your hearts.

SPIRIT OF TRUTH, LOVE AND PEACE
(I CAN BE YOUR OASIS IN YOUR WILDERNESS)

January 6th, 1991
Epiphany

O Holy Spirit of Truth,
descend upon us and be our
Guide and Holy Companion.

---

[1] That is: The Holy Spirit.

Holy Spirit of Love,
come upon us and teach us
to be in the real Love of God.
Remind us the True Knowledge,
this knowledge the
Father had given us, but
that we lost because of our sins.

Holy Spirit of Peace, give
us Your Peace -
a Peace the world cannot give.
Make out of each one of us
vessels of Light and
"peacemakers so that when we
work for Peace we will be
able to sow seeds which will
bear fruit in holiness."[1]
Amen.

Beloved, I tell you solemnly that I, the Holy Spirit of Truth, provide you day and night, night and day, with considerable graces to help you all on your way to perfection. Since I am your Life, allow Me to direct you and be your Guide in this exile you are living in. I can be your Oasis in your wilderness - O how little do you know Me! Creation! You spend your whole lifetime, creation, seeking your happiness in futile things, when I, Omnipresent, offer you Love, Joy, Peace and Freedom to free you from the dungeons of evil. My Graces are multiple yet you are unaware of My Presence and of how many graces your spirit can obtain from Me. I ask from My faithful ones, prayers, for the salvation of souls. All will vanish one day, all will wear out like a garment but

---

[1] James 3:18.

your soul remains forever. The Harvest is ready and soon the Reaper shall come and reap His Harvest. Be prepared for the Reaper.

THE SPIRIT IS ACTIVE AND ALIVE

January 24th, 1991

Peace be with you. Beloved, you whom My Heart seeks to attract without ceasing, you whom My Heart loves to folly, you whom I created out of My Sublime Love, you whom I made out of your body, My Temple, live holy... And you who sin constantly, offending Me, My Heart has forgiven you. Rejoice! Be joyful! For your Master is not far away, your Lord is on His way of Return. Come and praise Me, come... Even the pebbles and the rocks will soon cry out on My Return: "blessings on the King who comes!" Whoever comes to Me, even in his or her state of sin and is repentant, I shall not turn away. Yet to this day there are some who do not believe in My Mercy nor in My Love - not only do they not believe but it is they who betray Me. Today I am telling you as I had once said: "no one could come to Me, unless the Father allows him."[1] This is why I am telling you to pray that all may receive through the Father's Mercy, Grace. Grace to be converted, yes, to "come" to Me. It is necessary that one be brought by Grace, given to him from above - I shall never reject anyone who accepts this Grace. So do not waste your time seeking objections to object My Spirit's Works - if I call and you do not respond, you are not

---

[1] John 6:66.

responding to Grace. Beloved ones, I ask you to pray that everyone receives this Grace to believe and be converted.

The Words I am giving you are Spirit, they uplift, they revive and they give Light in your inner darkness. I have, children of Mine, given you many signs to believe that the Spirit is active and alive - so do not wait for material signs. My Spirit comes with full force in these days to help you now when night is yawning its darkness all around you. How My Heart pities you to watch your little hands grope their way through this night! I am giving you many signs that you may believe that these are the days when My Spirit is being poured out on all mankind as never before. So you who still waver, distrustful and doubtful, asking Me to give you a sign to show you that these Messages, among others, spread in the world are from Me, I tell you again most solemnly: it was not Moses who gave your ancestors bread from Heaven but My Father. It is He who gave them bread from Heaven - it is My Father who feeds you, for the Bread of God[1] is that which comes down from Heaven and **gives life to the world.** Your ancestors ate manna in the desert and I have given the multitudes already a forerunner of My Eucharist. I had multiplied the loaves to feed them, as I feed you My Body, to give you Life. I had multiplied the fishes too, a symbol of My Name, a symbol of He-Who-Feeds-You, a symbolic sign of My Name, **ΙΧΘΥΣ** which means Jesus Christ, God's Son and Saviour. So I tell you most solemnly today that the Messages My Spirit is outpouring on every nation, are not merely words, they are Spirit and they are Life. Have you not read what Scripture says: "He gave them bread from Heaven to eat." (Exodus 16:4) Are these signs not enough to convince you?

---

[1]Jesus now means the Holy Spirit.

Today I am feeding your interior desert with a Celestial Bread, still another miraculous food, a Miraculous Food that does not perish but enlivens your spirit. For as the earth makes fresh things grow, as a garden makes seeds spring up, so does My Glorious Food reactivate in you **Life**, ardour and devotion. Like a spark that can give fire so does My Holy Spirit come down on you to reanimate this flickering flame inside you into a consuming Fire of Love.

Scripture says: "an unspiritual person is one who does not accept anything of the Spirit of God, he sees it all as nonsense. It is beyond his understanding because it can only be understood by means of the spirit." (1 Corinthians 2:14) The New Heavens and the New Earth are right at your doors now, yet many of you have not understood and see it all as nonsense. These unspiritual people prefer to take all of My Signs in a superficial way and scorn My Celestial Messages, but Scriptures are being fulfilled, for they had indeed announced that during the last days there will be people who will make fun of My Promise. Since I knew that men have an infinite capacity for sinning and that the Enemy would be enthroned in the end of times into My Sanctuary, I have, for this reason, kept for Myself a remnant to be the builders of My New Sanctuary, the First-Fruits of My Spirit. As I had once kept for Myself seven thousand men who had not bent the knee to Baal in those days of Elijah, today too I have by My Grace kept for Myself this remnant, a hundred and forty-four thousand people[1], all with My Name and My Father's Name written on their foreheads.[2] These are the ones who never allow a lie to pass their lips[3] - these are My first-fruits of the

---

[1]Symbolic number: from all around the world, a perfect people. (Apocalypse 14:1).
[2]Apocalypse 14:1.
[3]Apocalypse 14:5.

New Heavens and the New Earth. These will be the trees[1] of life which would bear twelve[2] crops of fruit in a year, one in each month, and the leaves of which are the cure for the pagans.[3]

To refresh your memories, I shall explain to you once more what the book of Ezekiel the prophet[4] says: "along the river, on either bank will grow **every kind of fruit tree**", this means: Spirit-anointed priests to laymen. "With leaves that never wither and fruit that never fails, they will bear fruit every month because this water[5] comes from the Sanctuary"[6] since this water will come and rise from the throne of God and of the Lamb and flowing crystal-clear, down the middle of the city street[7]. "And their fruit will be good to eat and the leaves medicinal." Like a tree you shall be, renewed by My Holy Spirit that never fails you and your leaves shall be medicinal. Yes, your witnessing shall cure the sick, converting nation after nation, but not on your own, it will not be you speaking but My Holy Spirit who lives in you. And like builders, I shall send you from the ends of the world with a cane in your hand like a measuring rod[8] to reconstruct My Sanctuary and the altars that lie in ruin and have become the haunt of the devils.[9]

Pray, My beloved ones, that everyone may have time to convert. Pray that Grace comes upon them so that they

---

[1]Trees of life = the new-born = the first-fruits.
[2]Symbolic number : The New Church. The People of God.
[3]Apocalypse 22:2. The new disciples who by means of the Spirit will go out to convert godless people.
[4]Ezekiel 47:12.
[5]Water coming out of Christ's Heart.
[6]Water coming from Christ's Heart.
[7]Apocalypse 22:1-2.
[8]Apocalypse 11:1.
[9]Apocalypse 18:2 - Altars, allusion to: souls.

recognize and acknowledge the Truth. Pray for those who have turned to myths rather than the Truth; pray for the conversion of the world; pray that I inhabit every soul and that I make her My Property; pray that I may flow in these souls like a river down the middle of a city street.[1] Sacrifice for these conversions. Little children, stay near Me for a leopard[2] is lurking very near by. Stay near Me in constant prayer, an infinite prayer. Allow Me to leave My Sigh of Love on your foreheads, blessing you all. Be one under My Holy Name.

YOUR HOLY SPIRIT WILL MAKE HIS HOME IN US
(A PRAYER FOR UNITY)

April 8th, 1991

I shall not allow your strength to crumble, I shall give you My Food as I always did. Flower, My Message this time is a prayer for all nations a prayer for unity. Come, write:

> Praised be the Lord, for the Celestial Food[3] you are giving us and this is to fulfil Scriptures and to complete Your Work. You have given Your knowledge to mere children and not to the learned, for this is what pleases You Lord.
>
> Praised be the Lord to have laid open roads so that your people walk in them

---

[1]Apocalypse 22:2.
[2]Apocalypse 13:2. Daniel 7:4-6. Hos 7:4-6.
[3]Holy Spirit, allusion to spiritual food.

and come to You and fill Your House, for
though You have sent Your Son into the
world and the world plainly saw the Light,
they have not all accepted the Light but
turned instead towards darkness, falling in
apostasy.   The world has apostatized
because they have refused the Truth and
preferred to live under a Lie. Yes Lord,
You so much love the world that You are
today, in spite of our wickedness, sending
us without reserve Your Holy Spirit to
enliven us and revive the world, renewing
every creature, so that everyone sees
Your Glory and believes and thus be
converted.

Praised be the Lord for opening the doors
of Heaven to pour out from Your
Reserves this Hidden Manna[1] reserved
for our Times. No, it was not Moses who
gave bread from Heaven, it was You,
Father, who fed the true bread, and as
Your Son Jesus Christ **is** the Bread of
Life, the Holy Spirit too nourishes us, for
all Bread that descends from Heaven **is**
Life. It is written in Scriptures: they will
all be taught by God[2] and flesh and blood
cannot reveal the Truth unless the Truth
is given by the very One who established
the Truth and imprinted It into our hearts.
 Father, may Your Name be praised
always and glorified again. Let the world
pass from Darkness to Light, from Lie to

---

[1]Apocalypse 2:17.
[2]Isaiah 54:13.

the complete Truth, from Lethargy to Fervour. Father, Creator of Heaven and Earth, the hour has come to show us the New Heavens and the New Earth where Your Holy Spirit will make His Home in us. Most Tender Father, as You glorified Your Son and Your Son glorified You, let Your Holy Spirit of Truth glorify again Your Son. In a short time, Father, according to Scriptures, the first heaven and the first earth shall disappear soon, to prove to the world that Your Word is something alive and active and that Jesus has indeed conquered the world. When that day comes, Your Son's prayer to You will be also fulfilled, for we shall all be one in You as the Holy Trinity is One and the same. We shall not differentiate ourselves under Your Name anymore.

Praised be the Lord and Glory to the Highest for sending us, in our great apostasy, Our Holy Mother whose Heart You Yourself united in love with Jesus' and who suffered together. And it is together again that the Two Sacred Hearts will renew us and bring us back to Life; and in You lost sheep will be found, wandering lambs shall be reminded of their true fold and their True Shepherd, this Shepherd who neither deserts his flock nor abandons the lost but heals the wounded and supports the weary.

Praised be the Lord in Whose Holy Spirit we receive baptism. Indeed, fountains of living water flow out and are given to the man who is thirsty since they flow out freely from Your Holy Sanctuary,[1] this Sanctuary which You raised in three days and from Your fullness we are receiving in these last days the Grace of Your Holy Spirit to revive us, for this is Your Manna from Heaven, the Spiritual Food coming from the Spirit. Let your people, Father, realize that the ban soon will be lifted and that the Lamb's and Your Throne will soon be in Its place and among us. Prepare us, therefore, Righteous Father, for this Glorious Day when we can praise You and glorify You all around one Holy Tabernacle.   Father, I thank You for hearing my prayer and for having given me Your Words to indicate to the world the Riches of Your Sacred Heart.   Amen.

THE INNER POWER OF MY CHURCH IS MY HOLY SPIRIT

April 15th, 1991

Lord, come to us in full force with Your Holy Spirit. For, most tender Abba, as You glorified Your Son and Your Son glorified You, the hour has come that Your Holy Spirit of Truth glorifies Your Son. Prove to the world that Your Word is something alive and active and not just printed

---

[1]Jesus' Chest (Body).

words on paper. Let Your Holy Spirit "turn the hearts of fathers towards their children and the hearts of children towards their fathers." Ml 3:24.

Peace be with you Vassula. Scriptures never lie. It has been said that in the last days to come, people will keep up the outward appearance of religion but will have rejected **the inner power** of it[1] Ah! My beloved, will there be any faith left on My Return?

The inner power of My Church is My Holy Spirit in it, alive and active, like a heart in a body, My Holy Spirit is the Heart of My Body, which is the Church.

The inner power of My Church is My Holy Spirit who gives freely and distributes its gifts and its graces so that the Church gets some benefit.

The inner power of My Church is My Holy Spirit, the Reminder of My Word, revealing nothing new but the same instructions given by the same Spirit.

The inner power of My Church is My Holy Spirit, that transfigures, uplifts and turns you into real copies of Myself.

The inner power of My Church is My Holy Spirit, this Fire which enlivens you, purifies you and makes out of your spirit columns of fire, ardent braziers of love, living torches of lights, to proclaim without fear My Word, becoming witnesses of the Most High and teaching others to look only for Heavenly things.

The inner power of My Church is My Holy Spirit, the Life and the Breath that keeps you alive and makes your spirit desire Me, calling Me 'Abba.' If you refuse, My child, and suppress the gifts of My Holy Spirit, **what services will you be able to do and offer Me?** Do not be like corpses that

---

[1] 2 Timothy 3:5.

keep up the outward appearance of religion but reject the inner power of it, with futile speculations thus limiting Me in My Divinity. Do not stop those who come as children to Me, living a life of devotion to the Holy Spirit, it is I who calls them to the wedding of My Holy Spirit.

The secret of holiness is: devotion to Me your God and you can do nothing of yourselves, unless My Spirit living in you guides you and teaches you Heavenly things. I tell you truly, whoever fears Me will accept My correction - so do not sleep now, for these **are** the Times when one should be awake and vigilant more than ever. These are the Times to open your ears and listen to My Spirit and not disregard it - do not play the sage at the wrong moment by pushing the Breath of My Holy Spirit aside and suppressing the inner power that activates My Church.

You want to be prudent? Open your eyes then. You want to be prudent? Open your heart and your ears, My friend, not your mind. A prudent person never scorns a warning from the Spirit, only the proud do not know anything about fear. The fear of the Lord is the beginning of Wisdom. You want to be prudent? Look for the Truth that desperately leans over your misery to save you! Look Who is bending towards your wretchedness and your wickedness to pull you to Him and lift you from your graves to breathe Life into you again! O come! Do not misunderstand Me, **I am not forcing you nor am I trying to violate your liberty!** I have taken pity on you generation. Do not say that all I had to say has been said - why limit Me as yourself?

I am the **Reminder of My Word**, yes, **the inner power of My Church** and I am **free** to send you new portents and do fresh wonders. I am free to raise you generation and pour healing ointment on you from the Riches of My Sacred

Heart, when I wish and on whom I wish. I am building, yes, re-building My Church that lies now in ruin. So do not let Me face you generation in the Day of Judgement and be obliged to tell you: you, you were one of My persecutors who pulled down while I used to build. Mercy is at your doors now and My Compassion knocks on your doors in your times of tribulations.

You say yourselves holy? Prove yourselves holy by showing Me your adoration to Me. Prove yourselves holy by showing Me the souls you are converting and bringing to Me, for My Kingdom consists not in spoken words, nor of **an outward appearance of religion**, but an Inner Power that only I can give you through My Holy Spirit, if you seek it. Feel My Presence and My Love I have for each one of you. I, Jesus Christ, am present and bless you all out of the depths of My Sacred Heart, leaving My Sigh of Love on your forehead. Be one. Ecclesia shall revive.

I AM SENDING YOU MY HOLY SPIRIT
IN THIS NIGHT
(APOSTASY CHALLENGED MY MERCY
- THE WOMAN CLOTHED WITH THE SUN)

May 6th, 1991

Look, look around you, My Holy Spirit comes to meet you and revive you all. Dressed as a beggar, with Tears of Blood streaming down My Cheeks, I descend from My Throne, leaning all the way to you, to save your soul from disaster and from famine. **For the sake** of My Holy Name I shall demonstrate Myself through these very things you do not believe anymore, I shall demonstrate My Holy Spirit through marvels, through miracles. I shall demonstrate My

Power through weakness and wretchedness as never before. I shall come with thousands of myriads of angels to pour on you, generation, My Celestial Manna, this hidden Manna[1], **and fill** your mouth with My Food so that your mouth proclaims My Glory. Apostasy challenged My Mercy, and Rationalism - this plague of your era - challenged My Power. I am sending before Me, to educate you, the Woman clothed with the Sun, the second Eve, to school you and lead you step by step into Heaven. I am sending you My Holy Spirit in this Night to be your Companion and Consoler and remind you of My Word. I am sending you a mission of angels of hope to expel your fears. Come and listen all you who are starved. Happy the man I invite to the Wedding of My Holy Spirit - he shall be filled with My Celestial Food and though their faults overpower them, My Holy Spirit shall blot them out in His rest in them. Understand, My beloved, that My visit on earth is not to condemn you, but to save you. Who is going to see Me? Who will take notice? Who will recognize the Throne descending from the Heavens among you? Do not resist My Holy Spirit of Grace, I am with you always.

Pray fervently for the conversion of your era, open your hearts and **speak to Me.** Will you offer Me your will? O House of Mine! Come, come to Me and walk in My Light. Yet, when I come in My Great Return, will I find any faith on earth? Today I am speaking in plain words. My little children, in a short time Love will return as love. I will come back to you and I tell you truly: if you recognized My Holy Spirit and have seen Him, it is because you belong to Me, since the world can neither acknowledge Him, see Him, nor receive Him. Ah My little ones what will I not do

---

[1]Apocalypse 2:17.

for you! I am longing to see you strengthened with the gifts I am pouring on you.[1]

**Receive your strength
in prayer,
a constant prayer to Me.**

I bless each one of you and **you**,[2] who came because your cross is crushing you, **lean on Me beloved** and offer Me your distress and your hardship. I love you, I shall come to your help. Glorify Me by praising My Name. Receive the Breath of My Holy Spirit on your foreheads and be one under My Holy Name.

MY HOLY SPIRIT WILL TRANSFIGURE YOU
(APOCALYPSE 21 EXPLAINED)

May 13th, 1991

My child, allow Me to speak to My children by giving Me your consent to use your hand and your time.

I am bound to You out of love. Lord, am I not Your Property? So use me fully and as You please My Lord, for this is my delight. Come Holy Spirit and invade me.

City![3] Whom I came to visit to proclaim My Love through you to all of you and to heal your sick inhabitants, I shall

---

[1] Jesus had paused there. Then, majestically, straightening then not moving, said these words.
[2] Jesus speaks specifically to one person in the group.
[3] God suddenly and unexpectedly changed tone and His Voice with great force cried out to me calling me City.

not let you perish in guilt nor will I wait to see you decay, I shall triumph over you. I am your King, I am the Perfect One. Hear Me: I intend to model you, generation, into a reflection of My Divinity. The sinner's brood I shall consume by a roaring Fire. Your generation will have her wedding with My Holy Spirit[1] and I shall, with My consuming Fire, change the surface of this earth into a divine, prosperous and new Earth, and the world of today will be gone. I shall turn you all with My consuming Flame as pure as gold and transparent as glass[2] because your hearts will be Mine and in Mine. I and My Father will be your Abode[3] and you too will be Our abode. I intend to give you back your divinity, creation, so that My radiant glory will be like a lighted torch[4] inside you. Then like a sentinel guarding a gate, I shall guard you too from anything unclean which may want to come inside you.[5] I shall make out of each one of you a radiant city: I shall renew you entirely for this is the way I shall have you ready to wed My Holy Spirit. My Holy Spirit will make His Home in you, transfiguring you to become His Holy City,[6] His Domain and His Property. The world of the present shall be gone and My Will on earth shall be done as it is in Heaven. Love shall descend as love and I, the unseen God, will become visible inside your heart - the hour is coming when you shall no longer grope your way in the dark, since your heart will be lit by My radiant glory.[7] My glory will become visible in your hearts. Come, My child, hear My Mother now. Remain near Me. We, us?

---

[1]Apocalypse 21:2.
[2]Apocalypse 21:21.
[3]Alluding to God Almighty and the Lamb were themselves the temple - Apocalypse. (Inside us, the 'city.')
[4]Apocalypse 21:23.
[5]Apocalypse 21:27.
[6]Read Apocalypse 21:1-3.
[7]Apocalypse 21:24.

Yes my Lord. I am seduced by You, seduce others too.

Intercede for them and I shall come and seek out and save what was lost.[1] Read Isaiah 41:17-20. Love loves you. **IXθYΣ** ⤲⬭

YOU ARE THE SANCTUARY OF MY HOLY SPIRIT
(THE CITADELS OF GOD)

June 2nd, 1991

My Lord?

I Am. Peace be with you. Soon, very soon now I shall strip off your old behaviour and your old self creation, to vest you with My Divinity[2] and remind you of the True Knowledge. So listen, My beloved ones, to My Holy Spirit - allow Me to prepare you all so that you may be ready to receive My Kingdom. I, the Lord, invite **everyone** to share with Me and see My Glory. My Heart is sick with love for your generation... Alas! for those who would still be carrying their sin, coiled inside them as with child when My Day comes![3] Pray that everyone may be ready when that day comes. Ail for your brothers who still live in darkness and **have flung My Glory for a worthless imitation**, this very one that the prophet Daniel speaks of.[4]

---

[1] Luke 19:10.
[2] Allusion to New Heavens and New Earth, Apocalypse 21:1.
[3] Allusion to Matthew chapter 24:19.
[4] To the unbelievers who do not believe anymore in the Perpetual Sacrifice: Holy Communion. The Resurrection.

I shall speak to you in plain words considering the state of
your soul and your lack of Knowledge. I do not come by
force upon you with My Holy Spirit to violate your liberty,
nor do I come to condemn you, I come to you out of
Mercy to give you freely the fullest Knowledge of My Will.
Through My Perfect Wisdom I come to augment in you the
Knowledge I Myself have given you. **I do not come to add
new things into that which has been given you already** but
I come to place My Kingdom in the middle of your hearts.

Citadels![1] Have you not yet understood? Have you not
yet understood that I, the Lord, live in you? Have you not
understood that **you are My sanctuaries**? When I speak to
you about Heavenly things are you ready to receive them?
Listen: Scripture says: "zeal for Your house will devour
Me." Indeed, today **again** My zeal has reached its zenith
and from above Fire shall come down and devour My
sanctuaries[2], I shall transform you, Citadels[3], into a state
of Grace in which you will no longer apprehend to desire
My Glory nor fear to admit My Divinity.[4] The Plunderer[5]
infiltrated like smoke in you, **you** who are the sanctuary of
My Holy Spirit, the sanctuary citadel of My Divinity.
Satan's smoke penetrated through hinges and holes,
invading you in your sleep, because you had not
acknowledged Me in My Divinity but rather followed your
own irrational ideas. I tell you this: I shall **fill** your darkness
with My Light because I intend to wed you, generation,
with My Holy Spirit.[6]

---

[1] We are God's house, a citadel for God. God called out to
us calling us "Citadels", Daniel 11:31-39.
[2] Us.
[3] That is: us.
[4] Here God means that the unconverted and the unbelievers who
refuse the Holy Eucharist and deny the Real Presence of
Christ in the Eucharist, God shall change with Grace.
[5] Satan.
[6] Apocalypse 21:2. Apocalypse 21:9-11.

It has been said that by force the Rebel will feed you one day a portion of Rationalism and the other day a portion of Naturalism with the intention to abolish and extinguish the little light that is left in you, **you** who are My temple. The Invader[1] has invaded many of My Citadels,[2] forcing his disastrous abomination[3] inside you and **abolishing My Perpetual Sacrifice**[4] from within you[5] to erect in its place a worthless imitation[6], an image of mortal man, which is an abomination in My Holiness.[7] You are My Holy City[8] and **you**, you who allowed My Holy Spirit to flow in you like a River,[9] you are My New Jerusalem[10], the First-Fruits[11] - those very ones who had constancy and faith[12]. And like dew coming from My Mouth, like raindrops on the grass, you shall put Hope in many arid hearts because all the radiant Glory of My Heart shall reflect in you, making you glitter like some precious jewel of crystal clear diamond.[13]

I tell you solemnly: many of you who are not born of the Spirit shall receive from above, by My Grace, the **Spirit of Truth**. The Spirit of Truth shall descend in all His radiant

---

[1]Satan.
[2]Us. Allusion to Daniel 11:31 - 'forces of his will come and profane the sanctuary citadel.'
[3]Sects like New Age etc... Materialism, rationalism that lead to atheism.
[4]Once these people fall into these sects, or into atheism, they also stop receiving the Perpetual Sacrifice which is the Holy Eucharist. Dn 11:31.
[5]Read Daniel 11:31-39 and Apocalypse 13:14-18 and Apocalypse 21:1-27.
[6]Sects: aping the Word of God.
[7]Jesus was weeping.
[8]Jesus said this very majestically. Apocalypse 21:2.
[9]Read Ezekiel 47:1-12. Apocalypse 22:1-2.
[10]Apocalypse 21:2.
[11]Apocalypse 14:4.
[12]Apocalypse 13:10.
[13]Apocalypse 21:11.

Glory out of Heaven and make His Home in you. My Holy
Spirit shall wed you to become His bride,[1] embellishing
you by His Holiness, and suddenly the Heavenly things will
become visible in your hearts and My Kingdom unseen yet
to the heart shall become visible and crystal-clear in all its
Glory.

Beloved of My Soul, Citadels, blessed are you that will be
found blameless.[2] (This[3] is My way of teaching you
Heavenly things - it is not without labour, My child, but be
reassured, all that I have to say shall be written and read -
this is Wisdom teaching you, My Vassula. I love you and
My love for you is everlasting).

I shall let everyone marvel at My first-fruits, and little by
little the old world will vanish[4] and wear out like a
garment.[5] Only a little while now and all that had been
covered shall be uncovered and all that had been hidden
shall be unveiled in front of your very eyes. My New
Jerusalems! **You**, who are the first-fruits of My Love, you
whom My Holy Spirit seduced by My New Hymn of Love,
you whom I wed - go out to the nations and sing to them
My New Hymn of Love.[6] Work for Peace - sow the seeds
I have given you. Be like trees growing by the banks of
the River of Life[7] - let your leaves be a medicinal[8] balm
for the wretched and let your branches bear fruit in
holiness. Be My breech-menders[9], restorers of My ruined
sanctuaries.

---

[1]Apocalypse 21:2. Apocalypse 21:9.
[2]Allusion to Mt 24:19-20.
[3]Jesus speaks to me now.
[4]Apocalypse 21:4.
[5]Hebrew 1:11.
[6]Apocalypse 14:3.
[7]Apocalypse 22:1.
[8]Apocalypse 22:2. Ezekiel 47:12.
[9]Isaiah 58:12.

Give to those who fell into Satan's impious nets and were fed portions of Rationalism and Naturalism and My healing Water from My Breast, this stream that flows out of My Sanctuary[1], will fill you and make you wholesome - no man shall be able to arrest this rivulet. The stream will keep on flowing profusely out of My Heart - it shall flow **everywhere**, breaking into several parts, separating into other and several rivulets going into all directions and wherever this healing Water flows, **EVERYONE**, sick, lame, blind, will be healed. Even the dead shall come back to life again. **No one** will be able to stop Me from purifying you. Ah! Beloved ones, from rebels, I shall raise levitical priests; from dishonouring Me I shall turn you into pearls, radiant cities of light to honour Me and I shall live in you because you shall be vested in My Own Holiness. I, the Lord, will be in the land of the living. And those who stifle My Holy Spirit and see everything as nonsense, I tell you: I have things that go beyond your minds, I shall demonstrate the power of My Spirit and make your lips open and your heart cry out to Me:

Abba!

Love shall perfect you. Wisdom shall teach you to acknowledge My Holy Spirit and I shall make you join the saints too. I bless each one of you, leaving My Sigh of Love on your forehead. Be one under My Holy Name **ΙΧΘΥΣ** ⤜▷ and you, who are My chosen instrument to bring My Love before pagans and rebels, continue your journey with Me. Allow Me to call you when I wish. I Am is with you and loves you. Come.

---

[1]Christ's Body (Heart) Ezekiel 47:12.

THE SPLENDOUR OF MY HOLY SPIRIT
(THE REBEL AND THE GREAT APOSTASY)

June 27th, 1991

Today, many of you are denying the outpouring of My Holy Spirit. The graces and the gifts My Holy Spirit is giving you out of My Infinite Generosity are ignored and suppressed. These peoples deny and reject all the gifts of My Spirit. Many go around keeping the outward appearance of religion but are rejecting the **inner power** of My Church, the inner power which is **My Holy Spirit.** They say: "I have kept My faith, all there is to come now is the trophy of My Righteousness." I ask you: have you done **everything** you can to present yourself in front of Me? I have been trying to awaken you and tell you that you are like a dried-up river, and that all you say is hollow and while the sinner is being converted by My Holy Spirit, no sooner does he enter My House, no sooner does he discover the Treasures of My Heart reserved for all of you, than you come upon him like a gale to tempt him back into godlessness. He who has just escaped from rebellion, you tempt him back to rebel. In the Day of Judgement I shall tell you: you have not believed Me, but made Me out to be a liar because you have not trusted the testimony I have given you about the Advocate, the Reminder of My Word, yes, **My Holy Spirit of Truth** - this very One you never ceased to **ignore** and persecute, never ceased to deny and suppress. Instead of joining the saints who acclaim and praise with blessings and shouts of joy My Holy Spirit, you hound them and persecute them unceasingly, clinging to your illusion of piety. You are provoking Me with your constant denials. How can I then not let the stones manifest My grief? You prohibit My first-fruits to acclaim My Holy Spirit, this is why I tell you:

if these keep silence the stones will cry out[1] My grief.[2] What I once said to Jerusalem I tell it to you now with sorrow: "if you in your turn had only understood the Splendour of My Message of Peace! but, alas, it is hidden from your eyes!" If you in your turn had only grasped the Splendour of My Holy Spirit, bestowing blessing upon blessing on all of you... but alas, you neither see nor hear the Advocate, the Holy Spirit, whom the Father sends in My Name, teaching you and reminding you of all the truths I have given you, because the prince of this world is using your freedom for your own downfall.

Lord, show Your Mercy to these too, and like You made me hear You, let them hear too; and like You showed Your Beauty to me, leaving me dazzled, show them Your Perfection too.

They are not listening - they are listening only to their voice. Even while My Tears flow before them there is no reply. I have gone in all directions to find a way of breaking through their deafness and tell them to come to Me and base their strength on Me, so that I in My turn lead them to holiness and allow them to inherit My Light. I am the Holy One they are so wickedly betraying and I am the first to forgive them had they one moment of regret... but as long as they maintain their stand of self-sufficiency they shall **not** hear Me nor will they be able to see how today I am revealing entirely and as never before My Holy Face to all the world.[3]

I, the Lord, shall keep on shining on you creation and I

---

[1]Luke 19:39.
[2]Divine manifestations of images and statues of Jesus and Mary shedding tears.
[3]Allusion to Joel 3:1.

shall spread across the face of this earth My Light - the sun that has darkened and the moon that lost its brightness[1] in your era, leading you in your darkness to apostatize. Soon, your distress shall be over. I intend to turn your marshlands[2] into a garden, the night into day, your cities[3], which are only a rubble now, into cities of Light. Your broken altars[4] will be rebuilt and of your temples[5] I, with My Own Hand shall lay the foundation. I shall make the whole creation new.[6] **I shall renew you all with My Holy Spirit**.

Come, Vassula, My lamb, all shall be written and as I want everything to be written. Love is by your side. **ΙΧΘΥΣ**

YOU HAVE MADE A CULT IN PERSECUTING MY HOLY SPIRIT TO THE POINT OF FRENZY
(I HAVE LITTLE TIME LEFT NOW BEFORE MY FATHER'S HAND STRIKES THIS GENERATION)

July 23rd, 1991

Greece - Rhodes

My Holy Spirit, My Vassula, shall go to the very ends of the earth and seek even the least amongst you to save you from the disastrous abomination that dwells within many of you now... The Heavens soon shall deluge at My

---

[1]Allusion to Matthew 24:29.
[2]Us.
[3]Us.
[4]Us.
[5]Us.
[6]Apocalypse 21:5.

Coming upon you. I, the Lord, have done many wonders for you **and shall do more in these coming days.**[1] Pray My child, pray for those who offend My Holiness and blaspheme My Holy Spirit calling My Spirit foolish. Have I not said: "...everyone who says a word against the Son of man will be forgiven, but **no one** who blasphemes against the Holy Spirit will be forgiven." (Luke 12:10) for the Spirit is not opposed to the Son, nor is the Father to the Spirit, since all three of Us agree[2]. Many of you are condemning My Celestial manifestations and persecuting those whom My Spirit speaks through them because you do not believe they come from Me.

Daughter, look at the Wounds of My Body[3]... **I have little time left now before My Father's Hand strikes this generation.** Listen to your Father from whom you are sprung, listen to His Voice:

> I went all ways, seeking to gather you and remind you to live holy since I am Holy, but only a remnant of you pay attention when I speak. I have spoken through those you call contemptible. I have spoken through weakness and poverty, **but you have made a cult in persecuting My Holy Spirit that guides them, to the point of frenzy!!** I have been sending you through them the spirit of Elijah and the spirit of Moses - those two witnesses dressed in sackcloth[4] - to prophesy and remind you of My Law,

---

[1] The fall of Communism in Russia after the 3-day putsch.
[2] 1 John 5:8.
[3] Jesus' garment was soaked in His Own Blood, His ankles which I could see had blood with wounds like stripes.
[4] Apocalypse 11:3.

before My great Return. They are to
speak to you in My Name and bring you
back to the truth and back to your
senses, but over you spread a heavy
darkness and your claims to your
knowledge became a **battlefield to My
Knowledge.** **The Lie was and is
persecuting the Truth** but Scriptures
never lie. It was said that "the beast[1]
that comes out of the Abyss is going to
make war on them and overcome them
and kill them."[2] Indeed, your battlefield
is drenched now with **innocent blood**
because My Holy Spirit of prophecy has
become a **plague** to those who belong to
the world.[3] Their frenzied persecutions
and total **rejection** they have for My
mouthpieces are similar to those of
Sodom; their **stubbornness** to open their
heart and comply, their refusal to open
their ear and listen to My Voice today
have gone **beyond** the stubbornness of
Pharaoh in Egypt.[4] Today I am giving
you "things that no eye has seen and no
ear has heard," things beyond the mind of
man.[5] All these things that lift your spirit
to call Me: Abba. My Holy Spirit is calling
you all to true devotion and to a better

---

[1] In this context God made me understand that beast meant lie.
[2] Apocalypse 11:7.
[3] God is alluding to Apocalypse 11:10: '...because these two
prophets have been a plague to the people of the world.'
[4] God is alluding to Apocalypse 11:8: ... their corpses will
lie in the main street of the Great City known by the
symbolic names Sodom and Egypt...
[5] 1 Corinthians 2:9.

knowledge of God Himself - that is why I am continually repeating the same truths given to you. I shall continue calling you until I break through your deafness, generation. I shall not stop calling you in agony, not until I hear from you the word:

Abba!

The new heavens and new earth are soon upon you.
IXθΥΣ ⫷◯⫸

MY HOLY SPIRIT IS THE GIVER OF LIFE
(YOU WILL LEARN TO LIVE A TRUE LIFE IN GOD - THE DAY OF THE LORD IS AT HAND)

September 19th, 1991

I shall pour out My Spirit on this evil generation to entice hearts and lead everyone back to the complete Truth, to live

a Perfect Life in Me your God.

But be brave, because there will still be a Fire before My Day - so do not fear nor be sad because without this Fire the world's face cannot change... and when it comes, it will show the world how wrong it was. It will show its godlessness, its rationalism, materialism, selfishness, pride, greed and its wickedness, in short, all those vices the world worships. No one can say that I have not been telling you the outset of My Plans. No one can say that I have been hiding My Plans from you.

I am The Truth

and The Truth will always open His Heart and expose to you His fervent Plans **as they are.** The Truth will always give you the choice of proving yourselves to Him. If I had not spoken to you, if I had not been opening **now** the Heavens to you, you would be excused, but I **have** been calling you day and night without ceasing. I **have** been sending you My angels to speak to you; I raised from nothing, wretched souls, and formed them into fervent disciples to go and knock on your doors and repeat to you the Words I Myself have given them. No, they were not speaking as from themselves, but were only repeating the Knowledge that I Myself have instructed them with. They went to you in their poverty and barefoot to tell you of the things that are to come, not adding nor deducting anything from that which I have given them - all they said was taken from Wisdom Herself.

Now, I solemnly tell you that when that Day of Purification comes, many will be sorrowful to the point of death for not having allowed My Holy Spirit of Truth to enter their house,[1] but have welcomed in His place the Viper, the Abomination of the desolation and shared their meal side by side with My enemy. They welcomed inside their house the one who apes the Holy One; they worshipped the Deceiver, who taught them to misconceive My Holy Spirit:

**My Holy Spirit, the Giver of Life and
The Inner Power of their soul**

He who breathed an active soul into them and inspired a

---

[1]That is: their soul.

living spirit. I tell you solemnly, My Fire will descend in this world quicker than you expect it to come so that those without sight of their sins may suddenly see their guilt. It is in My Power to bring this Day forward and it is again within My Power to shorten this Hour, for this Hour will bring so much distress that many would curse the hour of their birth. They would want the valleys to open and swallow them, the mountains to fall on them and cover them, the vulture to devastate them quickly. They would want to dash themselves to pieces but no one will escape from this Hour - those that truly love Me will suffer only for not having done more for Me. They too will be cleansed. But woe to those who rejected Me and refused to recognize Me, they have their judge already. The Truth that was given to them will be their judge on that Day.

You heard Me say many times from My mouthpieces that

"the Day of the Lord is at hand"

and that My Return is imminent. If you love Me you would be glad to know that My Holy Spirit will come upon you in all His force and in all His glory. If you love Me you will continue to pray for the conversion of all My children who are unaware and still live under Satan's power. If anyone loves Me as I love you all, he will listen to Me and will remain faithful up to the end of his ministry. My little children, if you loved Me you would perform even greater works than those I performed while on earth but no one has performed anything greater yet because of the so little faith you have in Me and the ever so little love you have for one another. No one yet has loved Me as much as I love you, but on the Day of Purification you will understand how little you have done because I will show My Holy Face in you.

You hear those Footsteps? They are Mine. You hear the sound of My Breath already? It is the sweet sound of My Holy Spirit blowing through your wilderness and your aridity. You felt a Breath slide over your face? Do not fear. Like the Dove's wings, My Holy Spirit touched you slightly while hovering above you.

O come! Come to Me and as Moses lifted up the serpent in the desert, I too will lift your soul up to Me and revive you! As I was lifted up in Heaven, you too will be lifted up to Me to be nursed on My Breast. O come to Me! Get thirsty again, thirst for My Everlasting Wells, thirst to be with Me, your God! I will without hesitation offer you to drink and turn My Water into a spring inside you, welling up to eternal life - for from My Breast flow fountains of living water, an inexhaustible Source. O come to Me! Hunger again for My Bread and you will not die! Today, as yesterday, I stand up and cry out:

> "If any man is thirsty, let him come to Me! Let the man come and drink who believes in Me!"[1]

My forbearance is great and although I know you are sinners and you have polluted the earth with innocent blood[2], if you come to Me repentant, I will forgive your guilt and your crime. I am an Abyss of Grace. Do not be afraid... do not fear Me. Fear rather the Hour if it finds you unaware and asleep. This is the Voice of your Father; this is the Voice of the Sublime Source of Love; this is the Voice of He who once said:

> "Let there be light!"

---

[1] John 7:37.
[2] There was a stress, that Jesus put in my mind, on abortions.

and there was light. Come to Me and I shall give you My Spirit without reserve. Do not be like the soldiers who shared out My clothing and cast lots for them at the foot of My Cross. Come to Me with John's spirit; **come to Me out of love**; come to Me to console Me and be with Me.

The Hour is coming when the world will find itself only in distress and darkness - the blackness of anguish - and will see nothing but night. Bewildered, they will call out to Me but I shall not reply, I shall not listen to their cry. Frenzied, they will blaspheme My Revelation, Wisdom and the Truth. The whole world will be inundated by distress upon seeing the

Ark of the Covenant
My Law.

Many will fall and be broken, rocked and shaken because of their lawlessness. When the heavens will tear open - like a curtain ripped in half, showing them how they flung My Glory for a worthless imitation[1] - like stars that fall from Heaven they shall fall, realizing then how Folly led them astray, how by trying to climb up to the summit and rival Me was only folly! When that Day comes, I will show the world how wicked it was, how they befriended the Rebel and dialogued with him rather than with the Holy One.

The hour has come when constancy and faith, prayer and sacrifice are vital - they have become an URGENCY!

My little children, you who are sad now will rejoice later

---

[1] Allusion to Daniel 8:11-12. That is, the Holy Communion.

on. Come, let us pray:

Father all Merciful,
raise me up to Your Breast.
Allow me to drink from the
Running Streams of Eternal Life,
and by this I shall know that
I enjoy Your favour.
O come and rescue me before
the Hour comes upon me.
Cure me,
for I have sinned against You.
Father,
Your Lips are moist with Grace,
Your Heart is a blazing Furnace of Love,
Your Eyes are Two Flames of consuming Fire.
O Father,
Your Beauty is Perfection in itself,
Your Majesty and Splendour leave even the
brightest of Your angels dazzled.
Wealthy in Virtue and Grace,
do not hide Your Holy Face from
me, when the Hour comes,
come and anoint me with the oil of love.
God, hear my prayer,
listen to my supplicating voice!
I must fulfil the vows I made You
Eternal Father,
although the current is opposing me,
I trust,
I know,
I believe,
that Your Arm will be there
to lift me and pull me out of this current.
O how I long to gaze on
Your Sanctuary and see Your Glory

in the Ark of the Covenant!
O how my soul languishes to gaze
on the Rider of the Heavens
who carries the Name:
Faithful and True
He who will sweep away iniquity
from the world,
He who is Just.
O come and cover me with Your Cloak
since Your Love is known for its generosity.
O Father! Do not brush me off
like I deserve because of my sins,
but help me. Provide me with my
Daily Bread
and keep me safe and away
from the Viper's fangs.
Make me heiress of Your House,
make me Your child of Light,
make me a perfect copy of the
Supreme Martyr, to glorify You
for ever and ever. Amen.

NO ONE CAN STOP THIS HOUR OF MY HOLY SPIRIT
MY HOLY SPIRIT IS YOUR GUIDE, YOUR HUSBAND AND YOUR MASTER

October 29th, 1991

My Lord, not everyone listens to these messages when I proclaim them. Is it possible that they have not understood? I am not only talking for myself I am also talking about the present apparitions and about others You

*have used as Your instruments in a supernatural way. I
will put it to You directly: how many in the high hierarchy
today lend an ear and are positive? How many?*

And how many of the high priests and scribes lent an ear
to Me and were positive, only yesterday? Vassula, there
is a remnant chosen by grace to believe. Scriptures say:
I revealed Myself to those who did not consult Me
(Romans 10:20) yet from the very beginning I have invited
everyone to My School;

**My Holy Spirit is your Guide,
your Husband[1] and your Master**

I tell you truly that soon I will gather all nations in a circle
of Love and My Spirit will dwell in you giving sight to the
blind, since the Light that will be given you is: My
Transcendent Light - but how hard it is for those who have
accumulated riches in their spirit to penetrate into My
Light! How hard it is for the wise to penetrate into the
Spirit and perceive Its depths! How hard it is for them to
enter into My Kingdom! I tell you solemnly, the rejects of
your society and those you call unworthy are making it
before these - yes! Those who could not tell good from
evil, those who could not tell their left hand from their
right! I have been and am still inviting **everyone** to sit at
table with Me, but many have not responded to My
invitation - they laughed and scorned at My Gracious Call
and caused others, who wanted to come, stumble by their
teaching. Compare all this with My parable of the
wedding feast (Matthew 22:1-14)

I will come back[2]

---

[1] Allusion to Isaiah 54:5.
[2] Second Pentecost: The outpour of the Spirit: Joel 3.

and they will tremble; they will tremble when they will realize Whom they were **rejecting** all this time.   They renounced My Spirit and allowed themselves to be guided by their own spirit; they renounced My Light for their own; they renounced My Heavenly Knowledge given by Wisdom for a second-rate philosophy and their own rational knowledge;

- they have apostatised -

Since they have rejected My Spirit, My Light and My Knowledge, I shall take away My Kingdom from them and give it to a people who can produce its fruit. I shall then welcome these people as My own and ask them to come with Me and keep house with Me - in fact this hour is here already. I have decided to draw near Me the disreputable, those that hang around on every street corner, the unworthy, the nothing of the nothings, the wretched and those who never knew My Name.   I will turn to a wretched lot who never loved Me and make a nation of Love out of the - a holy nation - and they will glorify Me. They will be called priests of the Living God, priests of the Amen, and in this priesthood I shall rebuild My Church - in these hearts I shall unite you all and My Body will rest. The hour is here, and no one can stop this hour of My Holy Spirit.

When you will see the world disintegrating under your feet, when you will look to your left and see tottering kingdoms and cities reduced into a heap of dust and to your right mountains tumbling, know that these signs are the beginning of the outpouring of My Holy Spirit. When you see My pupils whom I Myself have formed, preach fearlessly in My Name, do not disrupt them - resist your temptation and discern the sound of their footsteps. I will keep sending you these saints to gather on their way all

the severed members of My Body, and no one, not even
the unclean spirits would be able to stop them - these will
instead fall down before them because they will know that
the Amen is their Master

the Amen is soon with you My child -
He who is your Consoler
and whose Home is in inaccessible Light
will eventually plunge you into His Light and absorb you.
- I am Love -

*Blessed be Your glorious and Holy Name, praised and
extolled for ever.*

ALLOW MY SPIRIT IN THE INNER ROOM
OF YOUR SOUL
(WHAT COULD I HAVE DONE FOR ALL OF YOU
THAT I HAVE NOT DONE? - OUR PERFECT UNION)

January 20th, 1992

Jesus, let Your Holy Face smile on us *and we shall revive.
Our division devoured us like fire.   Since You alone
perform marvels, bring us together and let men renounce
their folly.   Your Plan is to unite us by unifying the date of
Easter thus bringing us reconciliation.   I am calling for Your
Divine Help.*

My child, bear joyfully My Cross.   Praise the Father for His
generosity.   Hear Me: the wicked may hope to destroy My
Plan of Unity but they will be heading for their downfall.
When I proposed Peace, universal Peace, nearly all were
for war - how can I take up their cause to defend them

when My Father's Hand raises upon them? The net they have spread now will catch them inside. What could I have done for all of you that I have not done? I have taken your faults on Myself, I have reconciled you to the Father and My Life I laid down for you - so what could I have done more that I have not done?

Vassula of My Sacred Heart, rejoice Me and **allow My Spirit in the inner room of your soul.** Allow My Spirit to breathe and dwell in the depths of your soul; leave Me free to shatter all impurities and imperfections that confront Me. My Vassula, although your soul will leap like on fire every time I will lift My Hand to shatter all that still keeps you captive, do not fear, do not run away in horror - allow Me to uproot in your soul all these infirmities. I shall come like a tempest inside you and carry out the decision of My Heart and that is your preparation for our perfect union.

I had said in the beginning that you will be My Net and My Target but then you had not understood the latter, you had not understood that in order to prepare you for this perfect union, I need to purify you and adorn your soul. I would have to bend My bow and set you as a **target** for My arrow. Oh what will I not do for you! No, it will not be without wounds and torments but then do not fight away the Holy One. Allow My Spirit to augment in you and My Divine Fire roar in your soul, you will be molten under the action of My Divine Fire. Do not lament then when I come to you like a hammer shattering your imperfections, do not ask your Holy One what is He doing? I am on My way to the inner room, **My** dwelling place and persistent blocks will not stop Me from proceeding - I shall burst them all with a tempest, I shall devour these rivals.

O Lord go in moderation!

I want to bring to completion your purification, therefore do not restrain Me from proceeding. You are so dear to Me so let My Tenderness envelop you - refuse Me nothing soul. I want to make out of you a docile instrument since My Presence will be felt inside you like a fire and like an arrow. Do not fear - I shall not break you, I shall only break My rivals; I shall only be combating inside you; I shall also be mindful of your frailty. I have formed you and ordained you for this mission to be My Echo - so allow your King to rule over you; allow your Sovereign to reign over you. Nothing will escape My Eyes. Every little impurity will be seiged by My Purity and annihilated and My Light shall continue to glow inside you and My Spirit shall flow in your spirit like a river. So seek My Holy Face untiringly and you will understand that I Am is smiling on you.

A ☧ Ω

SURELY YOU HAVE ENOUGH RESPECT
FOR MY HOLY SPIRIT?
(MESSAGE FOR THE GREEK PRIESTS)

February 18th, 1992

Lord, I will not let my eyes off You, lest I fall again in apostasy.

Allow me to worship You at Your Footstool. O Lord, display now Your Power on us all. Bring upon us all Your Tempest that will whirl away our sins. Let Your Fire (the Holy Spirit) come upon us to enliven us and purify us. It is hard to cross this treacherous desert in the dark.

Maranatha! Come!

Peace My beloved - do not be in terror, My decision has been taken. I shall ravage the earth with My Purifying Fire and I shall carry out My Plan sooner than foreseen, the time of waiting is soon over. As for you, My child, do not be intimidated by Folly - turn your eyes towards Me and lean on Me, I am your Strength.

Look! Pray for your priests[1], pray that they may turn to Me and draw from Me: resourcefulness, Peace and Love. Many are decaying and very fast too. Pray for those[2] who play havoc with My blossoming flowers[3]. Tell your priests[4] that if among them there are a few who are still alive, it is due to My Tears - I water their faith with My tears, so I weep in agony to keep this remnant alive. **My Church is crumbling like rotten wood** and all I hear from them is:

'Is there a drought?'

They flout piety, they list bitter accusations against the Works of My Holy Spirit and allow their mouth to condemn them! The hour of darkness brought the Hour of Adoration to nil - worse still, they have established a monopoly of ostentation and presumption. I, their Lord, stand before them and ask them: "Why do you scorn the consolation that I give to My children today through the smallest part of My Church?" The Heavens will wear away soon and you are still unaware and in deep sleep. I shall come to you like a thief without telling you at what

---

[1] The Greek Orthodox priests.
[2] The Greek Orthodox priests.
[3] The newly converted Greek youth. Converted through our Lord's messages.
[4] The Greek Orthodox priests.

hour to expect Me[1]; I am asking you now with Tears in My Eyes, tell Me: What happened to My flock? Where are My perennial pastures? Why are My sons and daughters in captivity? Where is the youth of today? Why has the fragrance I had given you turned into a stench?, I weep over you, I weep over your excessive pride.   Your excessive pride made My Church resemble a gaping grave but you too will be subdued. My Fire is close now; I will bring you down from your glory... and when you will ask 'what happened?' I will tell you then: "My Kingdom has been taken from you and given to a people who will now produce its fruit"[2] It is the Spirit who gives life - surely you have enough respect for My Holy Spirit? Then why do you offend My Holy Spirit by persecuting Him? Judge for yourselves what I am saying - why are your young people separating from Mother Church to follow a second-rate philosophy? You have done well in remembering My Holy Spirit so constantly and in maintaining the traditions just as I passed them on to you, however, you speak without love and you are **blinded** by your zeal! You have lost the insights of My Mysteries because of your zeal! Have you not read: 'there is a remnant, chosen by grace - by grace, you notice, **nothing therefore to do with good deeds**, or grace would not be grace at all!' (Romans 11:5-6) I love you all but it is not without suffering, because you are objecting to My Holy Spirit's gifts - you are not objecting to a human authority, **but to Me your God.** I am reminding you of one last thing: one day you will see Me face to face and I will ask you to give Me an account of the way you looked after the souls I had entrusted you with. Today still you are making Me out to be a liar because you do not believe any more the testimony I had given you all about the Reminder of My Word!

---

[1]Apocalypse 3:3.
[2]Matthew 21:34.

My Holy Spirit

Wash your hearts clean and the heavens will shine on you. From above, I have been watching you, City of Tradition - you have practised the exact observances of the Law of My Primitive Church, but today you are blinded by ostentation and pay little attention or none at all to the weightier matters of My Law, Mercy! Love! Humility!

and a spirit of Forgiveness.

My sorrow is great and I groan inwardly as I wait for you to seek for the greater gifts of My Spirit; I am weary of seeing you preach spiritual things unspiritually. Had they understood the depths and the weightier matters of My Spirit today they would have accepted the gifts too of My Spirit, but the pride that you take in yourselves is incessantly lacerating Me. I have entrusted you with thousands of souls to teach and help them **gently**, drawing them into My Heart, reminding them of **My Tenderness**, **My Love** and My great thirst for them but you pass premature judgement on them and load them with burdens that are unendurable, burdens that you yourselves do not move a finger to lift! In My days I was the stumbling block and today My Holy Spirit is again the stumbling block for many of My sacerdotal souls. The Eyes of the Lord, I am telling you, are not only turned towards the righteous and the virtuous, My Eyes also turn towards the wretched and the ones you call unworthy. The stars from the sky will soon drop to the earth and the powers of heaven will shake and you will **still** be unaware. This earth will soon disappear and the new heavens and the new earth will be upon you and you will **still** be running away from My Spirit. Yet, if even today you humble yourselves and **sincerely** admit you are sinners and unworthy, I shall take away the spirit of lethargy that is hovering over your nation!

You say yourselves rich, show Me your riches then -
'Famine' is the only word I hear from your country;
'famine' is written all over you. If you say yourselves rich,
then where are your glorious pastures? Why do I stumble
on decaying corpses? How is it I hear no sound from you?
My Holy Spirit in His Infinite Mercy descends now to feed
you all and fill your spirit with My Celestial Manna. As a
Shepherd I shall look for My strayed sheep, I shall tend
their wounds with everlasting Love, I will support the
weak and the weary and those you pasture no more, I will
console My children - so do not hinder Me or become an
obstacle in these days of Mercy, **do not contradict what
you teach on My Spirit**. I have told you all this now before
My Day comes. Will I hear: 'God, here I am! I am coming
to repent! I will stop insulting Your Spirit of Grace
because I know that if I do, I would be severely punished.'
It is for your salvation that I speak and if I reproach you it
is because of the

greatness of the Love I have for you.

IXθYΣ ✝⟩ Vassula, pray for your priests to learn
real humility from Me.

THE HOUR HAS COME, THE HOUR OF
MY HOLY SPIRIT TO GLORIFY MY SON'S BODY

June 17th, 1992

*Yahweh my God, You who are so tender and so close to
me hear the sufferings of He who is the Delight of Your*

Soul: Jesus Christ, Your Son. The Church's gateways are all deserted and her priests groan for her desolation. The City once thronged with the faithful sits in loneliness as if suddenly widowed. Your temples[1] are perishing one after the other as they search for food to keep life in them but what they inhale instead of incense is Satan's smoke. Where are the domains like a garden? Where are the blossoming vines that gave out once, their fragrance? Why are Your altars broken?[2]

Peace My child, peace... hear Me: the Great Day is near you now, nearer than you think. Altar, tell everyone that I will show My Glory and display My Holiness through and through; I will pour out My Spirit without reserve on all mankind. Your eyes have seen nothing and your ears have heard nothing yet. Today your hearts are sick and your eyes dim because you are living in darkness and desolation and the Enemy roams to and fro in this desolation. I, the Lord, will multiply the visions on your young people and many, many more of your sons and daughters shall prophesy - more than now. I will make up for the years of your aridity that led you to apostatize; I shall send My Spirit without reserve to invade My domains and with My Finger I will rebuild My broken altars; and My vines with faded leaves looking now like a garden without water, I shall come to them to irrigate with My Spirit. I will remove the thorns and the brambles choking them, and My vines will yield their fruit. I will do all these things to save you. I will display portents in heaven and on earth as never before; I will increase the visions; I will raise and increase prophets; I then will send you My angels to guide you and I the Holy One will live in your midst.

---

[1] We are the temples of God.
[2] The three questions concern the soul. Domains, vines, altars, are our soul.

My people are diseased through their disloyalty.   They refused the gifts of My Spirit because they trusted in their spirit, not Mine, making treaties with their mind; but now the hour has come, the hour of My Holy Spirit, to glorify My Son's Body.

Come, Vassula, I want you zealous, I want you to love Me.   So My child, I will instil in you fervour and a few drops of My burning Love to enliven you with My Flame.

ANYONE WHO BLASPHEMES AGAINST MY HOLY SPIRIT WILL NOT BE FORGIVEN

September 7th, 1992

Faithfulness is the essence of Your word and Your word is integrity itself.   Our life is in Your Hands, and yet our liberty is ours.   It is Your Gift to us.   But what have we done with our freedom?   We used it to ensnare ourself and made out of it a destructive weapon for our soul.   We need Your Holy Spirit to intervene, that ever-flowing Source of River water let it gush now on us.

Ah Vassula... the paths of this generation will, in the end, be straightened and men will be taught faithfulness and integrity - just wait and you shall see...   As long as you live and there is breath in your body, I will shepherd you; I will keep instructing you in the fullness of My Wisdom; I shall guard you against stumbling. I, the Most High, have favoured you - be happy soul, be happy! Listen now and understand: there is no poison worse for the soul than the poison of blasphemy to My Holy Spirit.   Anyone who blasphemes against My Holy Spirit will not be forgiven - so be on the watch that you may not find yourselves blaspheming against My Holy Spirit. That is why My Wisdom says to you: beware not to apostatize and reject My Holy Spirit of Truth who descends to you in these days to revive your lethargy.

In My days on earth they hated Me for no reason, yet on the Cross I asked the Heavenly Father to forgive them. Today if the world rejects My Holy Spirit of Grace and mocks Him calling Him evil or foolish they will find themselves unrepentant when My Day comes. You who received a share of My Holy Spirit once, would fall from Grace and you shall not be renewed a second time. How would you, since you would be unable to repent with your heart and I will be coming and will still find you unrepentant, with your heart hard as stone, dry and without fruit..?[1]

I will have to cut you and throw you to be burnt.

Therefore, in all truth, I tell you, **open your hearts** and understand how My Holy Spirit blows anywhere He pleases, and breathes freely in My envoys. Recognize them by their fruit and do not be slaves of your mind. Every soul should know how mockery, jealousy, carping criticism, judgement and calumny opposes the Holy Spirit of Truth. You should be awake and praying not to be put to the test.

I say this to you today: if your lips should cause you to sin, fast then with your lips[2] rather than have your lips

---

[1]Jesus suddenly stopped here then very gravely said the following words.
[2]Jesus means to give a vow of silence.

condemn you and your soul burn with agony.[1] You must love your neighbour as yourself. You will say now: but You have given us this command already; yes, I have, but have you followed it? Pray and ask for My Holy Spirit to come and rest on you!

Vassula, let My Holy Name be always on your lips and in your heart. I am your Educator and My favour is upon you. Console Me and let your heart be My heaven; realize who I am. Pray with joy and I shall court you; praise Me and I shall envelop you with My imperishable Light; bless Me and satisfy My Heart and I Myself shall come to you and carry you across My threshold into My House. Yes, just like a Bridegroom carrying his bride across the threshold, I too will come delicately with great tenderness and love and carry you to show you My Throne of Glory.

I have sent you My Holy Spirit from above to rest on you and teach you what you have never heard of, to save you and millions of others. Remain near Me, My sweet disciple, our journey is not yet over, we still have a mile to go to teach the rest of My children the knowledge of holy things.

I shall deliver you to many nations to honour My Holy Name and on you will be written My Knowledge; I shall grant you to speak as I would wish you to speak. Let now your heart rejoice and treasure what I have said to you, never fail Me. Love Me and absorb Me. I am Love.

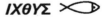 *IXθYΣ*

---

[1] Jesus means in purgatory.

ASK MY SPIRIT TO HELP YOU, ASK!

September 17th, 1992

My child, trust Me. You are unable to lift your little finger on your own - all power comes from Me. Reward Me now and offer Me your will - I am waiting.

My WILL IS YOURS!

I, Jesus, tell you: you enjoy My favour, for you are under My authority. Tell all those whom My Heart selected that I shall never fail them - the Spouse will provide their needs. Let everyone see in them true witnesses; let everyone know there is truth in them by their way of sharing. I am sending them out to face the world; they must abstain from carping criticism so that their tongue does not kill them or divide them; not one of them has earned this grace, I Jesus, offered them freely the grace, so no one should ask for money; the strong should support the weak, the rich the needy. As I have said, "there is more happiness in giving than receiving." *(Acts 20:35)* I will give you enough to cover your expenses so do not ever put Me to the test.[1] Be united in Me and among you; never give way to despair in your trials; do your best and I will do the rest! Courage, pray so that you may not sink; reveal the Riches of My Sacred Heart and My Glory to the world.

You want to be witnesses of the Most High? Die then to yourself; you want to be one with Me? Detach yourself from the world. You want to serve Love? Follow My

---

[1] Jesus means that no one should owe money to anybody or to any place.

Footprints drenched in My Sacrificial Blood.[1] Remember
one last thing: to be set free from your human inclinations
and weaknesses, **ask** My Spirit to help you - **ask!** and it
shall be given to you. I am gentle and humble of heart and
I know everything in your hearts, so ask My Spirit and My
Spirit **will** come to your help; the Spirit now asks you to
pray often this prayer:

> Jesus, neither death, nor life,
> no angel, no prince, nothing that
> exists, nothing still to come
> not any power or height or depth
> nor any created thing
> will ever come to separate
> me from You. I vow to
> remain faithful to You -
> this is my solemn vow.
> Help me keep this vow forever
> and ever. Amen.

... Up daughter and thresh! Let your thoughts be My
Thoughts; abandon yourself to Me so that all you do will
be done in My Spirit and according to My Mind.   Allow
My Spirit to breathe freely in you and I will accomplish My
Will in you. Happy are you My child, who meditate and
allow My Wisdom to be your personal Teacher! for She
will reveal to you many more secrets.   Receive and give,
give!

---

[1] Here Jesus asks us for _real_ sacrifice.

MY HOLY SPIRIT IS THE ZEST OF YOUR LIFE

October 5th, 1992

Father, once, before Your Majesty revived the memory of my poor soul, I had forgotten who had made me. The next moment You restored my memory You asked me to lift up my eyes to the heavens, then a ray of Light shone on me and like a consuming fire, Your Spirit rested on me. True Light, Inexhaustible Treasure, You are awe-inspiring, and stupendously Great! How can I not thank and praise You, most Tender Father for resting Your Spirit on my wretched soul and making Your Spirit one with me?

Peace be with you. It is I, Yahweh, your Eternal Father, the One who taught you with Wisdom; I am the Holy One who approached you in your misery and healed you; I spoke to you in your sleep and from thereon the scales of your eyes having dropped you have seen the Light. I have taught you, daughter, not to fear Me, but to fear Me only when you reject Me and rebel against Me; I have taught you to dwell in confidence in My Presence showing you My Infinite Tenderness and the Fatherly Love I have for each one of you. I Myself have plucked your sins by the roots and in their place with the space given Me, I planted My graces in you. Although your soul leaped like on fire I had to continue My route in your soul and overthrow all the rivals who kept house with you; in My Jealous Love I replaced those rivals with abundant fruit and henceforth I became your table-companion, your delight! Listen now, My daughter, My Own and write and tell My children this:

From the depths of My Heart I call to you **all**! Blessed are the ones who have ears to hear; if it were not for My prophets, can you then name Me who foretold the coming of My Son? If you say you live by the Truth and in My Love, how is it then that your generation today cuts out My prophets and persecutes them just as your ancestors used to do? Out of My Infinite Mercy a City is being rebuilt for My Own people - will this City renewed be rebuilt on the blood of those you will eternally persecute?

Today more than ever I am sending you My Holy Spirit to renew you, yet for how long will this generation keep resisting My Holy Spirit? Tell Me, can a body live without a heart? Learn that My Holy Spirit **is** the Heart of the Body which is the Church; learn that My Holy Spirit is the Breath of the Church, the Essence of zeal for Me your God; My Holy Spirit is the sweet Manna of Heaven nourishing the poor. Happy the man who opens his heart to My Holy Spirit - he will be like a tree along a river, yielding new fruit every season, with leaves that never wither but are medicinal. Happy the man who opens his heart to My Holy Spirit, like a crystal clear stream My Spirit shall flow like a river in his heart, renewing him, for wherever this river flows, life springs up, and joy!

Have you not read: the River of Life, rising from My Throne and from the Lamb will flow down in the middle of the city street? My Holy Spirit will shy away from malicious souls, but will show Himself openly to the innocent, to the poor and to the simple. With great joy My Holy Spirit will envelop these souls and become their Holy Companion and their Guide, and as they walk, their going will be unhindered; as they run, they will not stumble, and should they drink deadly poison they will remain unharmed; should they meet a legion of demons on their route, they will go by unscathed. My Holy Spirit will teach them the sweetness that exhales from Me, the depths of My Eternal Love. My Holy Spirit will take the innocent and make a pact of Love and Peace with them, to become fit and become His partner. My Holy Spirit will lift them and carry them - like a bridegroom carrying his bride across the threshold, He too will carry them behind the walls of the sanctuary where lie fathomless riches and mysteries, mysteries that no eye had seen before; and like a Spouse adorning His Bride with jewels He too will adorn them with imperial knowledge to delight in throne and sceptre. O what will My Holy Spirit not do for you!

My Holy Spirit is the zest of your life, the Royal Crown of Splendour, the Diadem of Beauty from My Mouth, the radiant Glory of the Living One, the Secret Revelation of your creation. My Holy Spirit is the flavour of your homilies in My Assemblies and the fulfilment of your Times... He is the Flaming Fire of your heart and the perception of My Mysteries; My Holy Spirit is the theme of your praises to Me revealing to your heart that I Am Who I Am, revealing to your spirit that I am your

Abba

and that you **are** My offspring, and My seed... Blessed be the pure in heart - they shall see Me. Rejoice and be glad and open up to receive My Holy Spirit so that you too may delight and hear My Voice! Open your hearts and you shall see My Glory, and like a child needing comfort, My Holy Spirit will comfort you whose love for you surpasses any human love.

I, the Creator of the heavens and earth tell you, My Holy Spirit is the Spouse of the Bride, of She who held the Infant Who was to save you and redeem you, and in Whom through His Blood you would gain freedom and forgiveness of your sins. He is the Spouse of the One Whom He found like a garden enclosed, holding the rarest essences of virtues, a sealed fountain, the loveliest of Women, bathed in purity because of her unique perfection.

My Spirit came upon Her and covered Her with His shadow and glorified Me making Her the Mother of God, the Mother of all humanity and the Queen of Heaven. [1] Such is the Richness of My Holy Spirit...

I am showering on all of you My Holy Spirit, now... today... I, Yahweh, the Almighty am telling you: I am giving you all this free gift to save you out of the greatness of the Love I have for you. Love and Loyalty now descend, I Yahweh lean down from heaven to embrace all of you; My saving help is offered from above to you - are you willing to comply with My given Law? Are you willing to entrust Me with your soul? Do not say I am unmoved by your misery and unresponsive to your prayers - if the flames lick up your countries and fires devour your people and if the inhabitants of the earth taste the disgrace of death it is all due to your great apostasy. You have shunned from My Holy Spirit - He who would have clothed you in blessings; He who would have made your heart and flesh leap and sing for joy to Me your God, but you preferred to become homeless, beggared and fatherless and today dwindling away in the shadows of death. How I pity you... O generation! How much longer can you defy Me?

My Love fills the earth, My calls fill the mouths of My envoys and though My grief is acute and My Justice is now brimming over I can still relent and I can accept the homage you would offer Me. I am ready to forgive you through the Blood shed by My Son and through His Sacrifice if you take My Words to heart. Soon, very soon now, My Holy Spirit will blow on you with such force

---

[1] I want to note that when the Father was dictating to me this passage concerning Our Blessed Mother, if He were not God, I would have said He was exalted, so much was His Joy.

making a mighty sound ring out at the four corners of the earth, as a reminder before all the inhabitants of the earth. Then immediately at the sound of My Holy Spirit's Breath, the people of the earth all together would fall on their face to the ground in adoration of Me the Lord, the Almighty, the Most High, and in the end the people would bow low before the Throne of the Lamb and receive the Blessing from the Throne and now, I who created you and I who formed you, ask you: will I deign to hear your cry of repentance?

DEMONSTRATE THE CONVINCING POWER OF MY HOLY SPIRIT

December 9th, 1992

Peace be with you. Favoured by My Father, be My Echo! Establish My Kingdom in Australia, sow My seeds of Love everywhere and in all directions; do not delay, and answer to all requests given you. I will give you enough strength to promulgate My Message... Demonstrate the convincing power of My Spirit; demonstrate how My Spirit uplifts, instructs and reveals the depths of the Truth and of the Eternal God; demonstrate to the unlearned the reality of spiritual things given by the Spirit and uncover the Knowledge given by My Spirit; demonstrate the full power of My Spirit, how He develops, testifies and gratifies the poor, the simple, the humble, but shies away from the rich, the wise, the proud who assess My Spirit with their natural understanding and evaluate everything in terms of

their spirit. Vassula, evaluate your spiritual growth and do not doubt of My grace. I, Jesus, am your Teacher and Master - never doubt. Ic,[1] have My Peace. *IXθYΣ*
⤳⬡

THE RIVER OF LIFE
(DO YOU WANT TO PASS THIS ERA'S THRESHOLD BY BLAZING FIRE? - WITH ALL YOUR HEART *HALLOW MY NAME* -)

December 13th, 1992

Since the foundations of the earth I have called you by your name but when I proposed Peace, universal Peace, nearly all of you were for war, yet I am pouring out My Holy Spirit now to remind you of your true foundations and that all of you are My seed - but today My seed is filled up with dead words... I am the Holy One who held you first - for how long will your soul resist Those Eyes who saw you first? and for how long will your soul deny My distressed calls? Many of you are still fondling the Abomination of the Desolation in the most profound domain of your soul. Can you not see how the Viper repeatedly is deceiving you in the same way he deceived Adam and Eve? Satan is suggesting to you, untiringly and subtly to cut off all your heavenly bonds that bond you to Me, **your Father in heaven**; he mesmerized the memory of your soul to make you believe you are fatherless thus creating a gulf between you and Me, your God. Satan wants to separate you from Me and cut off your umbilical cord that unites you to Me in which Rivers of Life flow

---

[1] Ic stands for short: "Jesus", in ancient Greek, usually on icons.

into you.

Generation, you have still not set your minds for Me - when will you decide to return to Me? Do you want to pass this era's threshold by blazing fire, by brimstone and devouring flame? How could your soul trade My Glory for a worthless imitation that the evil one offers you daily. Ask Me for **your daily bread** and I shall give it to you! Why are you all so willing to listen to the Viper? You and I know that Satan is the father of lies, then why are you still listening to him? I, your Creator, am your Father and I am calling you back to Me; believe in My distressed calls. Will your soul continue to befriend the Rebel, or will you deign to come down from your throne and repent? It is for you to decide - there is not much time left.

I am reminding you to beware of the false teachers and the false prophets who induce in your soul desolation and misinterpret the gospels, telling you that the Holy Spirit is not with you to remind you of your foundations nor of where you come from. They have already made a desolation out of your soul and dug a vast gulf between you and Me your Father - do not let them expand this desolation in your soul and mislead you into believing I have left you orphans. These false prophets have made out of My Son Jesus, a liar and out of the gospels an echoing cymbal, empty with emptiness. They made out of My Word a gaping grave - so beware of those false teachers, who tell you that My Holy Spirit cannot descend to perform in you miracles and wonders. Beware of them who condemn My Holy Spirit, who in your days more than anytime, reminds you of your foundations. Beware of them who keep up the outward appearance of religion but reject the inner power of it, the inner power that is My Holy Spirit.

Allow Me, your Father, to bond you to Me; allow Me to touch your soul. Come to Me and thrust yourself into My Arms. What greater bliss than being held by those Hands that created you? Place your ear on My Mouth, this Mouth that breathed in you through your nostrils: **Life**, and from the dust of the soil I revived you to conquer the earth; I touched you and asked you to listen to My Word since then. Come, you must set your heart right, renounce the iniquities that stain your soul and with all your heart

HALLOW MY NAME

THE SEAL OF THE SPIRIT

December 21st, 1992

Let them pray and say these words:

O Lord, You who stand among us,
shepherd us.
Set Your Royal Throne in
the middle of Your vine
and give us Your orders.
O Holy Lord of all holiness
purify us
so that we preserve the integrity
of Your House and Your vine.
Lovingly intervene and protect

what Your right Hand cultivated.
We have failed You
but we know,
we believe,
and we trust,
that You will open wide Your
Gateway
to let the River of Life flow
on Your vine;
and once more from it will
sprout branches that will
bear fruit and become a royal vine,
more kingly than ever before, because
Your Holy Spirit
the giver of Life
will overshadow it.   Amen.

and you, My Vassula, your sufferings will teach you to be patient.   Have you not heard that patience brings perseverance and perseverance brings hope? and this hope, upon this hope will raise My Kingdom. Let every part of yourself now glorify Me.

My Holy Spirit marked you with My Seal, so do not be afraid. Pastors, priests, teachers, bishops and cardinals will recognize the Shepherd's Call and I will renew their mind so that their old self is crushed and they will fully realize that I am on My way back to transfigure the whole of My creation in the goodness and holiness of the

Truth.

Come, My daughter, My precious one, I Am is with you.

AS FOR YOUR NATION, I WILL MELT IT DOWN
AS ONE MELTS IRON - WITH FIRE

January 6th, 1993

Jesus? Beloved One of the Father, my country's[1] fields are ravaged[2], they have now become the haunt of the lizard and the spider - are You no longer there? Are You no longer in this nation? Why does it make no progress? Why are You leaving them far behind? Death has creeped in under their doors... Son of the Almighty God, when will You display Your Holiness in this nation? ..."Vassilia mou, yiati kles?"[3]

I weep on her excessive pride... How am I to deal with their excessive pride? They do not listen to My Spirit and are following the dictates of their own proud hearts.

Truthfully, Lord of all Holiness, am I not doing my best to serve You, am I not interceding for Unity? Can I bend iron with my bare hands?[4] Your Fire though can do it. Your wealth and Your Treasures of Your Sacred Heart can do it.

Then I will have to ask more from you... I will have to ask more from you. All that you give Me will be to bind you all together in love, and enlighten your hearts so that your spirit may open to My Spirit who will teach you the depths of your Father in Heaven, and the hidden jewels of Wisdom.

---

[1]Greece.
[2]Spiritually.
[3]Greek: "My King, why do You weep?"
[4]The iron rods of my vision representing the three Christian Churches.

Poverty is at Your Feet, to serve You Almighty One.

Yes! Trust Me. I will always uphold you, so do not fear... Look at Me... My palate is dryer than parchment and the Father will not bear this sight much longer; the world is offending Him and His whole Kingdom. The world has become so wicked and My Arm cannot much longer hold away His Arm from falling upon you...[1] Iron can be melted, so do not lose courage... do not forget that I have posted you with a sword in your hand, to flash like lightning. For the proud, these News I have given you to carry, displease mightily their heart. They trouble their spirit and cause their knees to tremble. As for your nation, I will melt it down as one melts iron - with Fire ... and they will advance into holiness.

MAKE MY SPIRIT ONE WITH YOUR SPIRIT
(MY MERCY IS GREAT, BUT MY SEVERITY IS AS GREAT)

February 19th, 1993

Peace My beloved - are you one with Me?

Make my spirit one with Your Spirit. Only You can do it Lord.

I am glad that you are conscious of your nothingness and that without Me you can do nothing. Lean on Me and I will attract your soul to Me; Love is near you and My Spirit upon you. Allow Me to continue yesterday's Message;

---

[1]Suddenly Our Lord stopped, and looked at me, as if He remembered something, then spoke.

hear Me: tell them that mercy and wrath alike belong to Me, who am Mighty to forgive and to pour out wrath. My mercy is great, but My severity is as great.

(God asked me to write this passage from Ecclesiasticus 16:11,12.)

You see daughter, I will soon reveal My Justice too. My Plan has a determined time; My Merciful calls have also a determined time. Once this time of Mercy is over, I will show everyone, good and evil that My severity is as great as My Mercy, that My wrath is as powerful as My forgiveness. All things predicted by Me will pass swiftly now - nothing can be subtracted from them. I have spoken to you of the Apostasy, Apostasy that bound[1] the hands of My best friends, disarming them because of its velocity and its measure; have I not said that cardinals will oppose cardinals and how bishops will go against bishops and that many are on the road to perdition? They have, in their endless battle, weakened My Church. Today this spirit of rebellion thrives inside My Holy Place. Do you recall the vision I had given you of the vipers crawling all over the Holy Sacraments of the altar? Have I not revealed to you how many of them oppose My pope?[2] And how they push him aside?[3] I have already given you a detailed account of the Rebellion inside My Church. My faithful friend, allow Me to stop here - we shall continue later on. Stay near Me and please Me.

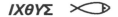

IXθYΣ

---

[1] It means they were helpless.
[2] Pope John-Paul II.
[3] Previous message.

BAPTISM OF FIRE
(MY WRATH IS AS POWERFUL AS MY FORGIVENESS)

February 22, 1993

*"Correct us Yahweh gently, not in Your
anger, or You will reduce us to nothing."*

Jr 10:24

Vassula, messenger follows close on messenger, to tell the
world to repent. I am manifesting Myself like never before
to bring everyone from far away back to Me and follow
My Commandments. At any moment this little flame
flickering inside this generation would die down if I do not
intervene; even to this day they refuse to hear and believe.
The greater they think they are the less they are in My
Eyes, how could they find favour with Me when they
obstruct My Holy Spirit? What I hear from them is: "Who
has authority over me?"   "I am self-sufficient."   My
compassion is great but My severity is as great. My wrath
is as powerful as My forgiveness. My temples[1] have now
a common ground with traders; they have exchanged My
Holiness for a tribute to Satan! I am speaking of those
who apostatised and have allowed a Lie to pass their lips
and now they intend to compel everyone to be branded
with that Lie and I am tired of bearing them. In My House
once, integrity lived there since My Law was their daily
bread, but look at what My House has become now - a
desolation, a haunt for the lizard and the spider! Ah... but
I will undo all this. My Heart is broken within Me, My
child, and My angels dread and tremble for the Hour I
reserved to break out when My orders will be given. I

---

[1] I understood: souls

cannot endure any more to see your Holy Mother's Tears shed over and over again every time My Son is recrucified; your generation's sins are leading My Son to Calvary every moment.

Together in one voice the world is blaspheming My Holy Spirit and all the powers of heaven. Daily, the world is provoking Me: "Look! Look what has become of the great Lord's House?" they say, while tearing It down and dissembling then. My Soul cannot bear any longer the groans of My Son being recrucified, although both My Son and your Holy Mother muffle as best they could their pain. My Ears hear everything; My Ears and My Eyes are not human and nothing escapes Me. Since it is your generation that makes the choice, not I,[1] the Rebellion in My House will bring down on you My wrath and the deepest Darkness is wrought on earth soon; it is not My choice but yours. I had chosen to lift you from your graves with Mercy and Love, Compassion and Peace, but look how so many of you are unmoved to My offer, nothing can touch you any longer.

My Patience you have exhausted and you, daughter, be My Echo. Hard as they may harass you, I shall not allow them to overcome you. On the contrary, you will be like a sword when you will pronounce My words; remind them again that I take pleasure, not in the death of a wicked and rebellious man but in the turning back of a wicked and rebellious man who changes his ways to win life. This earth that you know 'will vanish soon!'[2] I have decided to hasten My Plan because of the great sins your generation conceives. All will vanish, all will wear out like

---

[1] That is: instead of choosing God's Peace we choose to pass into the new era by God's Chastisement.
[2] Heb. 1:11

a garment.[1] This will be My way of destroying the defilement of sin, and you will realize that from the beginning you were My sacred temples and that My Spirit was living in you. Ah! for this Baptism by Fire!! Pray and fast in these last days. I Am is near you.

I ENCAMPED YOUR SOUL
(GO TO THE DRY BONES)

March 1st, 1993

*'Lord, when Your words came to me, I devoured them. Your word is my delight and the joy of my heart, for I was called by Your Name, Yahweh, God Almighty' (John 15:16). I had my eyes veiled and I did not see You nor Your Splendour nor Your Glory. Suddenly, in the deepest depths of my obscurity a Light shone! Stupefied and stunned by Its brightness I staggered, ...and the spirit of lethargy encamping my soul, overwhelmed by **Your** Spirit, ceased breathing in me.*

I saw You standing there, silent ...and it was as if I knew You, Beloved. Then, You opened Your Lips, a Name was given me, and instantly the memory of my soul was restored; the veil from my eyes dropped and I found my soul succumbing into my Father's Arms. O God! How Precious You are to me!

---

[1]Ap. 21:1 and 4

I am Holy. I said: I shall cleanse you and give you a new heart and put a new spirit in you; I shall remove the spirit of lethargy from your soul and put My Spirit in you. On that day I swore to make you Mine, I swore to heal you and like a tree, bear fruit for My people; I swore to fill the starved and every mouth. Yes! I swore to come to you, and turn to you to till you and sow in your Nothingness My Glory; and now I, God, encamped your soul forever. So prophesy without fear; go to the dry bones and I will give them flesh, I will give them breath to praise Me and glorify Me. Yes, I will breathe on the dead so that they live and shout: "who is like unto God?" I will remind them that greater love than their Creator's they shall not find.

SANCTIFY ME WITH YOUR HOLY SPIRIT
(AND NOW I WILL NAME YOU AFTER MY PASSION - VASSULA OF JESUS' PASSION)

March 2nd, 1993

Peace be with you. Every minute of your life consecrate for Me, the Sacred Heart. Today, My Vassula, I tell you: live as though it is your last day on earth -you must do everything you can to live holy. Any infringement of My Law from your part will be a horror in My Eyes! - have you understood, My Vassula, a horror ... Subject to sin, do not ever abandon My rules - every offering given with love to Me will be used for the salvation of souls. Subject to weakness, lean on Me and trust in My Eternal Power - be rooted in My Sacred Heart to obtain strength and light. Look, have I not favoured you to reveal My Face to you and to show all the Treasures of My Sacred Heart? This Glory of My Church? And by revealing My Face to you I have revealed It to millions of others. Jesus is My Name

and you are Mine forever, and now I will name you after
My Passion: **Vassula-of Jesus' Passion**. And now,
Vassula-of-My-Passion, pray with Me for this time of Lent
is going to be heavy on Me; address yourself to the Father
and say after Me these words:

Eternal Father,
may Your Name be hallowed.
To know You is eternal **Life**,
to know You is to know the **Truth**.
Father of all Wisdom, sanctify me
with Your Holy Spirit so that
my heart will utter sayings full
of wisdom.
Unique and Perfect,
source of Sublime Love,
Your Majesty, ravish my heart to
praise You night and day.
Fountain of Myrrh and Aloes,
fragrance my wretched soul
with Your delicate fragrance so
that when I meet My King and
Your Beloved Son,
He will not turn His Eyes away from me.
To know You is to be in Your Light,
this Light which will show me
the **Way**,
and draw me in Your Beloved
Son's Footsteps.
Well of Living Water come,
come and immerse me your child
in Your Stream that flows profusely
out of Your Sanctuary.
O God! I love You to tears!
Let my wretched soul long for
all that is Holy;

let my soul taste Your Tenderness.
Yahweh, You are my God;
I praise Your Name,
for You have looked upon my wretched
soul and filled it with the
brightness of Your Glory.
My heart now sings to You Father;
my spirit rejoices in Your Spirit.
O God, my Father,
allow my soul to succumb in Your
Loving Arms
by setting Your Seal on my heart
so that my love for
You becomes stronger
than Death itself. Amen.

Be like a spring, My child, to water arid lands.

God Almighty, allow my soul to take root in You. I have found true Peace in You Father.   Yahweh, my Lord, Sovereign from the beginning - evening, morning, noon - I love, I thirst for the Holy One whose Finger touched my heart and with one single of His Glances ravished my heart. Lord, I stand before You now, pitiful to look at, prisoner still of this wilderness. Come to my side, for so many persecutors ransom me...

Be like a tree that is planted by water springs - unattended you are not. I Myself am Your Keeper.

Loudly I cry to my Saviour now,
Jesus!
Sacred Heart!
You who have plunged my soul in a baptism of Love, do not let my soul fail You!

I am your Keeper too.[1] I am known to defend the poorest and save them from their oppressors. To you My Cup I have passed to drink it with Me... do you know why I have come to you? Do not be afraid, peace be with you. I have come to you to pour out on this generation, through you, My Infinite Love; I have also come to remind you that the Prince of Peace is coming - by the road He had left He shall return. I will come is as certain as the dawn. I have also come to tell everyone what is written in the Book of Truth[2] and explain to you in simple words what you have not understood. My Father favoured you to bear with Me the Cross of Unity and Reconciliation and cross this desert with Me, side by side; the Almighty has done great things for you. I will make My Voice be heard everywhere in spite of the oppositions.

Listen, Vassiliki, on account of the impressive wounds done to you by your accusers, who in reality are My accusers, your compensation will be great in heaven - I cannot spare you that favour.[3] My Justice will rise to its peak with these traders,[4] for indeed they are those traders who apostatized My Church; they have traded the Truth

---

[1] Jesus now answered me.
[2] I understood, the Scriptures.
[3] Jesus means that by allowing them to attack me, they do me a favour because heaven will repay me, compensating me.
[4] <u>Traders</u>: My Canadian accusers, in this context. <u>Traders</u>: Persecutors of the Holy Spirit. <u>Traders</u>: Symbolically meaning: "the jackals" working by "night". <u>Traders</u>: Can represent the second beast of the Apocalypse 13, meaning ecclesiastical freemasonry. <u>Traders</u>: The rationalistic spirit, apostatized and dry. <u>Traders</u>: Biblical term for a person who traded the Truth for a Lie. It also means: the spirit of rebellion, the false teachers and false
....continued over page prophets of today that Jesus warned us of in the last days to come. St Paul said: "Therefore we teach, not in the way in which philosophy is taught, but in the way that the Spirit teaches us: we teach spiritual things spiritually. (1 Corinthians 2:13).

for a Lie. My Eyes see everything and My Ears hear everything. I have seen horrors in My sanctuary by those very ones who accuse you; pray for their souls, My child - deceit is their principle of behaviour. **Oh no, they have not reconciled**; they never pause to consider that I know about all their wickedness! Their hearts are blazing like a fierce flame in the excitement of their plot to consume you together with My Messages - they conspire together.[1] It is daughter, only self-interest that makes them want to drown My Voice that comes through you! Fraud and oppression fill their mouth; they may bend their bow and take aim at you, but the weapons they prepared will kill them one after the other **unless they repent** and make peace with Me. I tell these traders: "your wealth will be seized... and, dressed in terror, you will sit on the ground naked. If you renounce all the sins you have committed, you will be forgiven - there is not much time left! Abstain from doing evil and return to Me - why are you so anxious to die Trader? I take no pleasure in abasing you, you who come from My House - repent and you shall live! The Hand of the Father is held out in blessing over all who seek Him. Trader - fast plead with the Father for His favour and He will listen."

And you daughter, I tell you: stand firm, be strong and continue to be My Echo; be like a double-edged sword and proclaim My Message with force and zeal; pray for the conversion of the world with your heart so that the nations recognize the Tenderness of My Holy Spirit - let them see My Love, My Peace, My Patience, My Mercy, and My Fidelity through these Messages. Be fearless and have in mind that I am with you and before you; embrace My Cross which will lead you to heaven; enliven My

---

[1] I understood that they are in one clan.

Church and delight My Soul. Go in peace and do your other minor duties; invite Me to share them with you. I, Jesus, bless you. Bless Me and praise Me. *IXΘYΣ*
✠

Blessed be the Lord. Praised be the Lord Jesus.

WHAT HAS BECOME OF THE SPIRIT WITH WHICH I ENDOWED YOU?
(I AM THE LIVING WATER AND IT IS I WHO KEEP YOU ALIVE - RESTORE MY HOUSE WITH LOVE)

March 19th, 1993

I was lingering this morning, then I saw the Lord and He said: "And when are you going to decide to come to Me?"

Vassula, I Jesus give you My Peace. Flower, tell Me, would a flower survive without water? No? I am the Living Water and it is I who keep you alive.

Sometimes Lord it is like You withdraw from me and leave me in the hands of Your and my persecutors. It seems like they have the power to put to death. Am I doing Your Will? Maybe I am not, maybe I am doing the opposite.

And do you believe I will permit it?

Sometimes You permit things that surprise us, and what we can only say then is: "well, God has His reasons. God allowed it to happen and frankly for us it is a mystery."

I am glad you are frank with Me. It is true that I allow

certain things to happen but they are for My greatest
glory. Since I and you made a pact of Faithfulness, I will
not permit anything to come between Me and you. I want
to heal this generation through My Sacrifice and to My Joy
I have found what I always wanted - I was looking for an
undivided heart and when I found your heart I decided to
conquer it ... (courage); I was out looking for an attentive
ear and I found it. Then My Wisdom has always been
given to mere children, as you know - this is why the
Father took pleasure in giving you Wisdom.

Is this true? (This was very spontaneous).

Do you doubt?

No!

The Father's Compassion is Great and although your
behaviour was just appalling, He overturned His enemies
inside you, and then made the scales of your eyes fall to
see My Beauty. And I, with all My Heart exclaimed:
Come! Come along with Me - I will prepare a table for
you. You will hunger no more and I will share My Cup
with you; My House will be your Home and together we
shall be on the road to conquer an irreligious people. I will
never hide My Face from you but you will also answer My
demands.

Restore My House with love[1] so that everyone recognizes
in you My reflection; let every lip say about you: "truly
they are God's holy people." And you, I solemnly tell you,
as I have said once before: if your hand or your foot
should cause you to sin, cut it off and throw it away - it is

---

[1]Jesus speaks to everyone.

better for you to enter into life crippled or lame than to have two hands or two feet and be thrown into eternal fire - open your hearts not your mind! Open to your King; allow Me to enter your heart and I shall fill your heart with joy!

Understand, My child, that your only weapon not to perish is prayer. I ask each one of you: who is truly seeking Me? Who among you would want to share My Cup? Cup of Division, Cup of Dissensions? I am seized with pain - your Saviour's Heart is lacerated so that it is beyond recognition.

When I will return how much faith will there be left? When I come will I find you, My friends, different from what I want you to be? Will you still have the language and the Traditions I passed on to you? Or will you be speaking like philosophers and preaching on a Tower of Babel? Tell Me - what has become of the Spirit of which I endowed you with? Your yeast is the same one as the Pharisees' and the Sadducees'; you talk of the Law but you do not carry It in your heart. My Law is alive! Men of little faith! But you have made My Word null and void by means of your spirit's reasoning. I tell you, your heart is as far from Me as the skies are from the earth, for you have neglected the weightier matters of the Law: love, repentance, mercy, good faith! Who of you who preach in My Name truly loves his enemies?

My children how hard it is to enter My Kingdom! My people, what have you done out of the language of My Cross? For how long must I put up with fraudulent teachings or that abomination you are erecting in My

Temple? See, today I am granting you to see wonders[1] -
even the pagans are beginning to see them[2]. For once
more I have taken pity on you; I, your God, am speaking
to you today - do not shut your door in My Face

...Of whom were You speaking to Lord?

of those who share My table ...and you, city of My
predilection, do not fret and wriggle in My Hands - let Me
govern you as I want to accomplish My Plan. Love
blesses you.

HEAVENLY FOOD GIVEN BY MY SPIRIT
(LET MY MANNA FILL YOUR MOUTH)

April 8th, 1993

*Lord, my God, You know that falsehood is not to be found
on my lips, You who can screen my soul and investigate
my sins, You know that I am innocent and not guilty of all
these accusations they are condemning me with. Have
You not endowed me with Your Spirit?*

My city! My beloved! I am the One who have driven you
to walk in My Footprints and in My Light. I have come to
tell you that you are not alone - see? My Arms are like a
wall of Fire all round you. To you, I tell you: do not seek
glory from men for whosoever is admired by men is
loathsome in My Sight. So let them hound you, let them
persecute you and do not fear My lamb, from those who

---

[1] The effusions of the Holy Spirit.
[2] Revelations and apparitions to non-Christians.

kill the body and after that can do no more. I will tell you whom to fear: fear him who, after he has killed, has the power to cast into hell. Bless Me rather for hiding still these things I have been teaching you from the learned and the clever and revealing them to mere children, for that is what pleases Me and delights My Soul! Learn that whoever touches you,[1] touches the apple of My Eye!

Do all you can, My Vassula, to present yourself in My Presence as a soul that has come through her trials with faith; show Me that you will stand firm as a tree, well-rooted in the Truth, Love, Faith and Hope and that when I will come to test your fruit I may rejoice! Prefer suffering than giving way to the weakness of your flesh. My child, no one will succeed to separate you from Me, so rejoice!

Alas[2] for the world that brings obstacles to My Message! And even more for the man who provides them! Vassula... I will show My Glory through you. Shall any of the hostile souls surround you, be to them like a double-edged sword that pierces the Lie.

Pray that this Heavenly Food given by My Spirit be distributed to the starved and the poor; let My Manna fill your mouths! And you[3], whom My Soul casts out as a net in every nation...,[4] "Imé stenakhoreménos para poli; avrio ine i proti stavrossi, ké pali, o Ios Mou tha ksana-stavrothi se epta meres..."

---

[1]That means, harasses me.
[2]God's tone suddenly changed.
[3]I felt God's Voice becoming sad and I felt Him sad.
[4]God spoke to me in my language (Greek), He said: "I am very sad, tomorrow is the first crucifixion, and again My Son will be recrucified in 7 days..." Because of the two dates of Easter.

I will dress the Heavens in black... Pray for the unification of the dates of Easter. Be in My Peace. I, Yahweh, love you. Proclaim My Word without fear! Come.

PROPHESY, AND IN THIS MANNER HONOUR MY HOLY SPIRIT
(OPEN A BROAD HIGHWAY FOR UNITY, MY FRIEND)

April 16th, 1993
Orthodox Holy Friday

I have been following Your Step ever since You revived me and by bowing my ear a little I have received You, my soul delights in Your Presence, I am in Your Loving Hands now, into the Hands of my God.

Peace be with you. Straighten the road for My Return; level My path on which I will tread; open a broad highway for Unity, My friend. My Return is imminent. Hear Me: today most of you judge by human standards - this is why your spirit is unable to fathom the Riches of My Heavenly Kingdom. Except a man be born again he cannot see the Kingdom of Heaven. Vassula of My Sacred Heart's Passion, dearest soul, I will encourage you by the same words My Spirit whispered in Saint Paul's ear: 'be ambitious to prophesy'[1] - this is what you will remind and tell My people. Tell them that one should be eager to

---

[1] 1 Corinthians 14:39.

prophesy and in this manner honour My Holy Spirit;

Lord, many condemn prophecy - I understand too - since there are many false prophets.

Men of little faith! How could you fail to understand what I have been teaching you? I have said that in the end of Times many false prophets will arise and you should beware of them, but have I not said that you will be able to tell them by their fruits? Why are so few following My instructions?

I am the Christ and I am sending you precisely for this reason, I am sending you to the nations to declare that My Word is alive! So stand your ground and do not waiver or fear, I am your Shield. Yes, My Vassula, I have given you the privilege not only to be in this special way with Me, but to suffer for Me as well. Do not ever doubt though that I am able to complete this Work by Myself; I suffice by Myself, but I have chosen you to perfect you. I tell you: your race is not yet over; I can assure you already that I will finish it with you. Go out to the nations and declare that My Law is alive and that I want to write it on their heart - so rejoice!

Rejoice and be glad for My Mercy is incomparable; be glad that Our Two Hearts, like Two Olive Branches, are among you to restore you to health and heal your wounds! Rejoice and be glad that Our Two Hearts like Two Lamps are guiding your steps into Heaven where you belong - to what can you liken My Mercy? And you whom I brought up and raised in My light, hold fast on to Me. I observe every action from Heaven, and I know that the most impressive wounds I will receive would be in the house of My best friends. I will have to drink of the Cup of your division, your unreconciled heart and of your apostasy...

spite and fraud is killing the innocent. No, My child, do not wait for thanksgiving or compassion from the world - but I too had received neither of the two on My way to Calvary. I tell your little heart: for the sake of My Love, I will increase My Calls and not diminish them; I will overpower every calumniating mouth, **for I am Lord**. Therefore rejoice, for by the wounds My friends inflict on you,

I will bring many back to Me,

I will let the blind see and the lame walk again - a great number of you will return to Me. Stop then your weeping and dry your eyes... My Vassula, come, ...I will wipe away your tears...[1] Soon the earth will shiver and shake and ah! so many will still be out in the wilderness erring... Come and lean on Me and trust Me. Pray because I delight when you remember My Presence - I love you dearly and unmeasurably.

I will always be with you.

IXθYΣ ><▷

THEIR SPIRIT IS NOT IN SEARCH OF MY SPIRIT
(TREASON AND LACK OF FAITH COVERS
MORE AND MORE THE CHURCH)

April 20th, 1993

Vassula My child, it is I Yahweh... I love you daughter. I will continue to send you abroad for My Glory - feel loved, protected, and guided by Me. Hear Me: time is nothing and means nothing to Me, so be prepared to face Me![2]

---

[1] Jesus changed tone and was speaking as though to Himself.
[2] I understood: The Purification.

A great sadness is in My Heart, for treason and lack of faith covers more and more the Church. Here are the words I hear from those who share the table of the Vicar of My Son: "how tiresome he is!" but, as I have once said to you, they are the Cains of your times and of those I have spoken of in My comments on the Ten Commandments. They pretend to go in search of Me with their incense in their hands, but their spirit is not in search of My Spirit. I tell you, they do not hallow My Name, no, they do not, they failed to appreciate My great Love; they defy Me daily and provoke Me by their unspiritual discourses; they deploy My anger with their sneers on My mouthpieces. Oh! but they will reel like shooting stars bound for an eternity of black darkness unless they descend from their thrones and repent! You must join to pray for them before My Day comes... Daughter, I bless you. Call Me when you wish, I will never fail you...

CHRISTOS ANESSTI!
JESUS WILL BAPTISE THE EARTH WITH FIRE

April 23rd, 1993

Our Blessed Mother:

I bless you, My child. Christos anessti!

Alithos anessti!![1]

Ecclesia will revive! Courage! Satan can put obstacles in your path but I am near you to remove them. When one decides for God one should leave everything to follow Him. All that you do is not in vain. Vassula, there is a baptism to come and what a great baptism that will be! **Jesus will baptise the earth with Fire** - until then I shall keep appearing; so now is the time of repentance; now is the time of reconciliation.

I tell you, dear children, the sacrifice God asks of you today is to **change your lives and live holy**. God is asking every soul to repent. Do not say that you are too wretched for God to forgive you, and that the Most High will not be compassionable anymore. God comes to you all, even to the most wretched; return to God and He will return to you; come and make your home in His Heart as He makes His in yours.

Let it be known that without earnest prayers you will not be able to see the Kingdom of God - His reign on earth is at hand. Remember - what God wants of you is a change of heart. Do not be afraid to acknowledge your sins. Live and practise the sacrament of confession. My children, I bless you all.

---

[1] Our Blessed Mother greeted me in Greek, in an Orthodox manner, after Easter: In the Orthodoxy we have as custom after Easter when one meets with another to greet each other by saying "Christ has risen." The other one replies: "He has truly risen!"

THE WIND BLOWS WHEREVER IT PLEASES
(BELOVED CHILDREN, YOUR HEARTS ARE STILL FAR FROM US)

April 26th, 1993

Our Blessed Mother speaks:

Beloved children, your hearts are still very far from us[1] because you have not yet understood the meaning of Our manifestations nor of Our words in Our Messages. You have not yet grasped the meaning of Peace, Love and Unity - if you had, your countries today would not be aflame. Had you understood Our Messages you would have understood these words of Jesus and would have put them into practice: "anyone who wants to be great among you must be your servant and anyone who wants to be first among you must be your slave" - just as Jesus came not to be served but to serve and to give his life as a ransom for many. Learn that the kingdom of Heaven is for everybody, but not everyone sees it and not everyone enters it - do not be astonished then if you see it given to others than yourselves.

God is now coming to everyone, but many of you do not believe - this is why there is no peace among you. God is free to choose the last-comers and enrich them with His Glory as much as He enriched the first-comers - has He no right to do what He pleases? Jesus said: 'the wind blows wherever it pleases.' Pray for Peace in your hearts; live as though it is your last day on earth.

I will take care that, after I will stop appearing, all of you will still have means to recall Our Messages and Teachings

---

[1] Our Blessed Mother means Jesus and She. The Two Hearts.

to memory, in the days of tribulations. I will not be appearing very much longer now, because the Sublime Glory of God's Presence will suddenly be among you - this is why you are all called into one and the same fold, the fold of the Lord Jesus Christ and into His Mystery. The Glory of God will be revealed to you all sooner than you expect.

Try and understand that Our Love is for **every one** on earth, so do not speak harshly dear children to one another, for God will repay with judgement those you are judging; as for the coming of the baptism of Fire, the Lord will come in flaming Fire to extirpate from the earth and burn to the root all the evil of this world that is sunk in vice.

Continue to proclaim around the world the Kingdom of God, and that Our Messages are meant to lead you to repentance. I, your Holy Mother, bless you.

EXCEPT A MAN BE BORN AGAIN
HE CANNOT SEE MY KINGDOM

May 6th, 1993

My child, I, Yahweh bless you. My Kingdom is for the pure in heart - it is they who see My Beauty! Anyone, My child, who cannot recognize My Holy Countenance now that I am speaking, are those of whom My Wisdom shies away; unless they become like children, nothing, nothing will ever be revealed to them. So pray for those souls who are blinded by their own wisdom - have you not heard that Wisdom will erect the poor and give them a place with the great? Pray especially much for those who say they "see" and judge My Holy Spirit in these Messages, for this is how they persecuted My Beloved Son and the prophets before Him. Except a man be born again he cannot see My Kingdom. Come, I give you My Peace. Trust Me...

MY HOLY SPIRIT, A TRUE INTERCESSOR
AND ADVOCATE CONDESCENDS YOUR CAUSE
(I AM REVEALING TO THE WORLD MY MERCY AND MY LOVE)

May 10th, 1993

O Yahweh, why are You so far from me again? Relieve this distress of my heart! Spare just a tiny glance for Your auxiliary slave!

Yahweh is My Name and it is Holy.[1] I give you My Peace. Vassula, your Father is speaking to you so that you, in your turn, repeat My Words to all nations, revealing My Holy Countenance, revealing all the secrets I have been whispering in your ear. I am revealing to the world My Mercy and My Love; I am coming to save the oppressed from the hand of the Oppressor and the Deceiver. Do not let your heart trouble you, my child - **lift** your downcast voice to Me again; you will pray and **I, your**

---

[1] I felt a rain of God's love pour on me...

Abba, will hear you! **Lift** your eyes towards Me, My child, and learn that I am your Defence and your Shield! **Lift** you heart to Me without fear out of the darkness and gloom surrounding you - I will not allow your heart to sink. Dearest child, you are not Fatherless - feel My Presence. I Am Who I Am is with you, so **lift** your spirit to Me with joy and delight at My Presence. Rejoice, for My Holy Spirit, a True Intercessor and Advocate will condescend your cause - so where are your oppressors aiming at?

Yahweh, my God, my words have been frivolous, but I can hardly pace with the Step of Your Beloved Son, Jesus. I fear to be behind in this work and lose sight of Him!

Do not fear. I want you to rely on My massive Strength. Go in peace.

HOLY SPIRIT, MY HOLY COMPANION AND FRIEND
(A PRAYER)

May 18th, 1993

Peace be with you. Repeat after Me these words:

Jesus my Light,
Jesus my Guide,
I love You because You showed me the Way.

Holy Spirit, my Holy Companion

and my Friend,
You who whisper in my ear
counsel, wisdom and consolation,
I love You, because You allowed my eyes
to see and hear.
I adore You because You resurrected
me and You became O Sweet Manna
from Heaven,
my daily Bread.
You have consoled my distressed
and wretched soul;
You care for me in this
desert, and You are mindful to my needs.
You are fanning into a roaring flame
Your Gifts to all mankind,
for the Glory of the Most Holy Trinity.

Give us all the grace to devote
ourselves to obeying Your statutes, and
that Your Law becomes
our delight. Amen.

Good. I love you and bless you. Your Beloved. Ic.

MY BLESSING SWEEPS ACROSS THE FACE
OF THE WHOLE EARTH
(REPENT, BECAUSE THERE IS NOT MUCH TIME LEFT NOW)

May 25th, 1993

*Eli! O Eli, my God, in your loving kindness come and
defend me! You who lifted me from the grave do not hide
Your Holy Face from me. Come to my side!*

Why do I feel You so far from me?

To many I seem an enigma, a phenomenon, but You Yourself asked me to be Your Echo - have You not? So why does Your Echo disturb their ears when I am proclaiming Your marvels openly? Is it Your immense Power that frightens them? Is it Your massive Strength that leaves them trembling? Is it Your Voice thundering from heaven around the earth, in every nation, and in every city, that torments them?

Is it because of Your majestic procession most powerfully revealed they are left in awe? Is it because I cry out at the four corners of the earth that Heaven is deluging soon at Your coming and that repentance should be made fast, that they, they are appalled? Or is it because of Your downpour of Blessings and Mercy they have doubts? Tell me, is it the Cries of Agony coming from a Father, that they cannot grasp?

Your cries of Unity, Peace and Reconciliation are resounding in heaven and on earth, yet who is listening? Who can understand? Their flesh is rotting under their skin, yet when You cry out, "Salvation!" no one listens...

Ah, Eli, so many are waiting that I may be seduced into error and head for my downfall for they have never understood how the hand of a sinner could be held in Your Hand.

*O Eli, they have never understood why You and I are running anxiously at each street corner awakening the dead, why this collaboration? And why am I sent at the crossroads of every city to announce **that Your Kingdom is at hand.***

So what am I accused for? Why am I feared and repelled? O Eli, they treat me as the scum of the earth; insult upon insult, calumny upon calumny, not that I care for my own name and reputation, but since I am guided by Your Holy Spirit, it is Your Spirit they are blaspheming. They are demolishing the Works of Your Spirit and knocking down whatever bricks have been reconstructing Your altars.[1]

O Eli, ever so Compassionate, why are You so far at times from me? Look! Look at how I am struggling in this desert and come and save me from those briars and thorns surrounding me, choking and tearing upon me! OPEN the way for me!

Am I to weep all day long for their deafness? Am I not human, so have I not the right to be weak, have I not the right to be sorrowful now and then? Has my heart not the right to fail me?

O Eli, for how long have we to wait until The Triumph? For how long must we wait? For how long yet will this Darkness last?

The Wounds of Your Son are unbelievably deep. The Tears of Your Son and of Our Blessed Mother have turned into Blood, so for how long Eli are You going to stand this sight? For how long are we to wait for this Triumph?

A conspiracy of traitors now have penetrated in the Heart of Your Sanctuary like vipers and adders, slithering in corridors they are waiting to strike the Truth and turn the Eternal Truth upside down and into Falsehood, by erecting their Disastrous Abomination into the heart of Your

---

[1]Altars stand for: souls.

Sanctuary to abolish the Perpetual Sacrifice of Your Son.

*Eli!   There is **no** Peace in Your House...   And soon darkness will cover Your House and like a widow in mourning, and bereft, Your House will wear Her black veil. So, are You **still** not going to intervene Eli?*

My Voice of Justice will be heard like a violent earthquake and these traitors will be struck on account of the evil done to My children, whose innocent blood is shed as a sacrifice. I will avenge My House, but the world will have to reap still what it has harvested. **I cannot forgive their guilt unless the world repents!**

I am sending in the nest of those vipers what I dearly love - I am sending you with My Word into the depths of iniquity; I am delivering you as My mouthpiece to spread My Message. So dearly loved by Me, wherever you pass, I, the Lord, shall leave on your traces a roaring Fire to consume the hearts of stone, extirpating atheism. I shall make them fall in My Arms, the Arms of their God - ah, and it will be terrible to fall into My Arms. In a flash I shall turn them into appointed disciples, and I shall send them to defend My Word and take up My cause. Daughter, as you have learned from Me, in this way I will teach the others too. I am now delivering among wolves what My Soul mostly delights in and dearly loves, to reveal My Holy Face.

Repent! Generation, your sins have dried up your soul. Why die, generation? Repent and you will live! **Repent**, because there is not much time left now - the Destroyer will reveal himself in these coming days, entirely! Oh Vassula! Whom can I urge to hear and warn? Whom am I to speak to and who will listen? Since everything is coming near the end now and the end is close, go and announce My Message even in every public square; go and widely publicize My Merciful calls... The yeast of those exploiting My House is powerful, so beware and keep your eyes open. Understand why I am sending My Son and your Holy Mother to patrol the world in your days - this is My Blessing sweeping across the face of the whole world. So raise all of you your eyes and when you do, you will see Heaven wide open and gleaming in all its glory - the Ark of My Covenant; the symbol of My Presence among you; the symbol of My Mercy and of My Salvation; the One who shows pity towards all of you.

MY HOLY SPIRIT IS THE HEART OF MY CHURCH
(ANYONE WHO IS UNITED WITH ME TAKES THE
SAME ROAD I HAD TAKEN - THE ROAD TO CALVARY)

May 30th, 1993

The Grace I have given you is so that I accomplish My great Plan on humanity. My Message will be like a Lamp shining on a lamp-stand, shedding its light in the darkness of your era, revealing in My Light, My Presence and My Beauty, revealing your God as He is:

Companion and Prince-of-Peace.
Eternal Father and Counsellor.

Come, continue to speak words of Knowledge. Be My

Echo...[1] Ah, one more thing, a simple reminder: I and you
are united; anyone who is united with Me takes the same
road I had taken - the road to Calvary; anyone who follows
the Supreme Victim becomes part of the Victim - you are
part of Me, a remnant of My Body... Offer your life in
atonement and come with Me in the valley of Death[2]; that
is where I will pour out My Spirit, that is where I will pour
out My Love to revive every dry bone - your work is in
that valley Vassula. I intend to overflow it with the River
of Life. I, who am the Resurrection and the Life, intend to
flower these dry bones of that Valley; I will show My
Compassion and My Love by raising the dead from their
graves leading them back into My House and with Me in
My House; their table will be full, their cup I will fill and
brim over **and** My Sacred Heart will be their Holy
Companion. I shall make one single Body out of all those
dry bones now lying scattered in the Valley of Death.
Yes, like in the prophet Ezekiel's[3] vision, I ask you the
same question: "Can these bones live?"

*No. Not without Your intervention. Not without Your
putting life into them, my Lord, for they are quite dry and
lifeless.*

I am going to revive them.

I am the Resurrection

I shall put sinews on them, thus the scattered bones will

---

[1]It looked like He was ending His Message, and as though He
remembered something He said: "ah!"
[2]Jesus means where all the spiritually dead are to be found.
[3]Ezekiel 37:1-10.

be joined together[1] then flesh will grow on them; I shall cover them with skin and give them breath, so that they live; I shall make out of them[2] one single Body... and bring them back to life again; I shall send My Holy Spirit to blow through Its[3] nostrils a most powerful Breath which will revive It and make It stand up once more on Its feet to Glorify Me; "I shall pour crystal-clear Water[4] over you[5] from My Throne to cleanse you from all defilement, and I shall pour out My Holy Spirit to live in your midst. My Holy Spirit will be given to you to become your Heart, then, I Myself will anoint this Body and the light I will give in your[6] eyes will be My Own Divine Light -it will be from My radiant Glory[7], and like a warrior you shall walk fearless for I will be your Torch[8] walking before you, showing you the way. You will need no lamplight, as I Myself will be your Light[9]. **All the other nations**[10] upon seeing your Beauty will follow your step, bringing their treasure and their wealth,[11] offering them together with themselves to you; and in your[12] hand I will place an iron sceptre dressing you in majesty and splendour...

This is how My Spirit will unite every single one of you in

---

[1] I understood that the Lord was speaking of our division, the division in the Church, comparing us to dry and scattered bones.
[2] The bones.
[3] The Body.
[4] Apocalypse 22:1.
[5] God speaks to the Body as all of us, His Church.
[6] Jesus speaks of His Church, the renewal of His Church, the New Jerusalem.
[7] Apocalypse 21:23.
[8] Apocalypse 21:2.
[9] Apocalypse 21:23.
[10] "All the other nations" means that, in the end every one will recognize Christ as the Son of God, thus Jesus' Prayer is accomplished. John 17:21.
[11] Apocalypse 21:26.
[12] God was speaking of the renovated Church.

the end[1] and every one will believe it was the Father who sent Me[2]. Every one will recognize Me as the Sacrificial Lamb.[3]

Show Your Strength now my Lord, You are all powerful, and come and UNITE Your Body. Your Holy Spirit has the power to renew us; come Holy Spirit and with Your Fire, melt us, since we are like stiff iron bars, unbending, come and melt us into one solid bar; melt our hardened hearts!

Ah Vassula! Increase your prayers for Unity - do not be tempted saying that I shall not hear you! Your prayers are like a thousand gems in My Eyes, a sweet melody in My Ears. Do not be amazed - I have set My Kingdom in your heart and I, your King, am reigning over you. I conferred Wisdom to you to advance you and others too, spiritually; I have been looking for someone to form with My Strength and thrust in the world, as one thrusts a net in the sea, to bring Me souls. Frail you are, but I rejoice in your frailty.

Listen now: **I will** melt you all![4]   I will put you all in a melting pot together, and as a fire stoked underneath the pot, I will melt you all down.   My Kingdom[5] shall not remain divided. Come - we, us?

Forever!

---

[1]Allusion to Apocalypse 6:15-17.
[2]John 17:21. Allusion to Apocalypse 6:16.
[3]Apocalypse 6:16. (The conversion of the world to Christianity).
[4]The 3 iron bars of my vision.
[5]The Church on earth.

MY HOLY SPIRIT IS THE CORNERSTONE
OF MY CHURCH

June 11th, 1993
Omaha - USA

My child, My child, I give you My Peace. Give Me the liberty to use your hand, give Me the liberty to use your lips, give Me the liberty to use your mind and your heart; allow Me to invade you - how else would you be My Echo to transmit My Messages if My Spirit would not invade your spirit? How would a branch of a vine live unless it gets its sap from the vine? Cut it off from the Vine and you will see how quickly it will wither.

My Holy Spirit is like a sap flowing inside you keeping you alive - this is the way, daughter, you should rely on My Holy Spirit, the Giver of Life, the Giver of faithful love, the Giver of joy and peace. Yes, My Holy Spirit is the Fire which bends and melts hearts to follow My Instructions, turning away your eyes from pointless images; My Holy Spirit is the generous giver of My Words making your whole mind and heart seek for Wisdom. Wholeheartedly entreat for the gifts of My Holy Spirit especially in these times - He will be your Torch to rescue you from Death and keep your feet from stumbling and oh! what would My Holy Spirit not do for you! My Holy Spirit will lead you to pass your life in My Presence and in the courts of My Kingdom. **My Holy Spirit is essential to reconstruct My Church**, He is:

The Cornerstone of My Church

but your generation is rejecting it[1]. I tell you again: the builders are there but they have to be formed and instructed. Hurry up and rebuild My Church by using every stone and do not forget the essential one, do not reject the cornerstone! and now, My child, repeat after Me:

> Lord, I am yours,
> save me and save my
> brethren too through
> your Redemptive Love. Amen.

THE SIGN OF THE SON OF MAN IN HEAVEN

December 23rd, 1993

Master, the fig tree will begin to form its figs, and the vines will start blossoming.

No, My bride, the fig tree has already formed its figs and the vines have already blossomed. Daughter, can you not see? Have you not noticed My Sign in heaven?[2] Hear and write: generation, I have been sending you and I am still sending you, My angels,[3] to gather My chosen from the four winds - from one end of heaven to the other - to stand ready because the Bridegroom soon will step out from heaven and will be with you. Your world of today will wear out quickly. I am sending you My angels to

---

[1] The Cornerstone.
[2] Allusion to Mt 24:30.
[3] Angels here stands for: messengers. The chosen ones sent by God to the world, carrying His Word.

gather My elect, My people, to renew My Church. Have
you not noticed? Have you not understood? Do you still
not perceive My Sign?

Today My Holy Spirit raptures one out of two, enwraps
him in His blazing Fire and sends him out to be a witness
to the Most High. My Holy Spirit lifts one while leaves
another one behind in the dust among dust. One is taken,
one left; My Holy Spirit like the wind, blows wherever it
pleases - you hear its sound but you cannot tell where it
comes from or where it is going. My Holy Spirit, like a
Bridegroom, appears in your days to court you, seduce
you and wed you. My Holy Spirit is laid like a precious
cornerstone in your heart to be the foundation stone of
your faith, of your hope, of your love and of your zeal for
Me your God. My Holy Spirit in your days blows on you,
this way and that way, His Breath is like a stream flowing
in every direction, and everywhere this stream flows fruit-
trees sprout up with leaves that never wither but are
medicinal, and everyone who eats from them is healed.
Yes, My Holy Spirit is a life-giving spring, the inner Power
of My Kingdom, raising disciples of Wisdom. My Holy
Spirit builds, renews and embellishes, but the Deceiver
destroys and batters to death all that is holy. How is it
that you cannot perceive the dazzling Light of My Holy
Spirit?

Like the light of seven days in one My Holy Spirit shines
today in heaven - is this Sign of the Son of Man appearing
in heaven[1] not enough for you? Like a shepherd
gathering his flock, My Holy Spirit gathers and saves the
dispersed flock. I am revealing things hidden and
unknown to you, generation, at the favourable time I am

---

[1] Mt 24:30.

revealing you these things. Whether you turn right or left
you will see the dazzling Sign in heaven of My Holy Spirit
and your ears will hear: "I Am He![1] I Am is with you in
heart; I Am is here to build your hopes, your strength, your
faith and your love. My child, "koumi!" Rise now you
who have perished long ago; rise now, My child, and take
your place; here is a shepherd's staff - I will direct your
soul to receive instruction. Go out now and look for the
rest of My strayed sheep; weary not on the way, My child,
and if you do I shall carry you on My Shoulders. Today,
I Myself will rally My sheep...

Ah, generation, how could you ask for more signs, more
than the Sign of the Son of Man that I am giving you
today? What man cannot, indeed, see My intentions? I
speak the Truth, yet you do not believe that it is I, who
speak - how is it you cannot grasp My Voice? Have you
ever asked yourselves how have the paths of those living
in the dust been straightened? Have you asked yourselves
who was it who opened the mouths of the dumb and gave
Wisdom's speech to the ignorant? and who was it who
instructed the poor in spirit, the wretches as you call
them? Have you not heard that My Holy Spirit is indeed
the Life-Giver? Have you not understood how My Holy
Spirit shuns in the presence of the proud of heart, but
reveals His intimacy to the lowly? My Holy Spirit today is
given to you as a Great Sign in heaven,[2] a reflection of
My Return.

So long as your thoughts remain earthly you will be unable
to grasp the things that are in heaven. Have you not read:
"Yahweh will appear above them and His arrow will flash

---

[1] Jn 18:6 and 8.
[2] Allusion to Mt 24:30.

out like lightning."[1] "See how Yahweh comes in fire? To assuage His anger with burning, His threats with flaming fire."[2] The works of My Father are being carried out. Listen and understand: I have said that I will be coming to gather the nations of every language. Many of you ask: "when is this going to happen and what will be the sign of Your coming?" I had forewarned you that when you would see the disastrous abomination, of which the prophet Daniel spoke, set up in the Holy Place, that is, when you see the Enemy[3] take his place where he ought not to be, and that is: in My Sanctuary, My Dwelling Place[4] - when you see this Rebel[1] claiming to be so much greater than all that men call 'god', so much greater than anything that is worshipped, **that he enthrones himself in My Sanctuary**[5] and claims that he is God, know that this was a foresign given before the Sign of the Son of Man appearing now in heaven to save you.

Lift your heads and look at the sky for My heavenly Manna, stand erect, hold your heads high, because your liberation is at hand. How is it that My Holy Spirit cannot be noticed among so many of you? The deep and the earth tremble at My visitation so do not say anymore that

---

[1] Zc 9:14.
[2] Is 66:15.
[3] The Antichrist; today there are many antichrists, for they have as their guide, the spirit of Rebellion which installed itself in the innermost part of their soul, there, where God ought to dwell.
[4] Dwelling place: soul.
[5] Allusion to Dn 11:31 and 8:11 and 12:11 and Mt 24:15 - as I said before, Jesus says to us that today already these signs are here: many antichrists, nevertheless, this prophecy of the Perpetual Sacrifice abolished, will come concretely: when the Apostasy and rebellion will be generalized, then <u>the</u> Antichrist, who is already among us will appear openly. Yes Vassula! (Jesus answered Vassula, approving what she had explained in writing).

justice is not being done, and that the Ark of the Covenant[1] is far away - the Ark of the Covenant is right above you in the sky so that you witness My Glory. If you eat from My Manna you will revive, you will be born again, so do not look for other signs. Have you not heard that it is the Spirit that gives life? If certain among you do not believe, it is because you have not eaten this Manna. Yes, it is My Holy Spirit who could give you an untarnished understanding to My mysteries. This heavenly food is the food of the poor and it is not bought with money.[2]

Sanctify yourselves and purify yourselves to enter the Garden, which is My Kingdom. I am giving you today this Sign of My Holy Spirit in heaven - it fills the whole world and makes all things new, deploying His strength from one end of the earth to the other, and yet, many of you defy My Mercy and venture to say: "where are the signs from God? There is no Sign of the Son of Man appearing in heaven to prove to us that Sovereignty is at our gates;" and you lie in wait for My Spirit-anointed-ones since they annoy you and oppose your way of thinking! Yes, the very sight of them weigh your spirit down. Ah... and the root of your understanding is decaying...

I tell you: My Holy-Spirit-anointed-ones may appear to you frail, but they are well rooted in Me; hardly grown, but they are grafted on Me and like an untarnished mirror I move them about, to flash My Words everywhere and

---

[1] Heb 9:4. The Ark of the Covenant contained a jar. Inside the jar was kept the manna that fell from heaven to feed Moses and the Jews while crossing the desert. Jesus makes an allusion to this manna to talk about His Holy Spirit: as Celestial Manna.
[2] The rich in spirit cannot receive the Kingdom of God. Allusion to the beatitudes: Blessed are the poor in spirit, theirs is the kingdom of heaven.

wherever they may be, **I Am.** And they will continue to flash My Words to you all, to lead you into My Kingdom. They will continue to reveal My Power even though you deal with them harshly; they will bear insult and calumny humbly to save you. They will not open their mouth to contradict you in the sight of all the nations, but will be like angels whose feet bring good news. They will continue to flash My Word like an untarnished mirror proclaiming Salvation and heralding Peace and Love and though they will be despised and rejected by many, they will bear their sufferings with dignity. Lift up your eyes to the heavens and discern My Sign. I am coming to restore My House; I am coming to renew you, generation; I am revealing My Holy Face to you all, to save you.

O come! you who still waver, I tell you: from the beginning I have never spoken to you obscurely, and all the time these things have been happening;

I have been always present.

And you, daughter, keep yourself untarnished so that My Light may reach to the ends of the earth. Preach with accuracy all that My Spirit is giving you. I will encourage you, My daughter and My Own - your Spouse is with you.

MY NEW NAME

November 9th, 1994

Vassula, ever so dear to us. Imitate us: I will continue to direct you and give you My instructions to be suitable for Our kingdom. During My instructions to you I will teach you to lay hands on your brothers and sisters so that their spirit falls in My embrace. The dead are going to be raised. I shall lift them, though not all. It is I who give you life and breath. Have you not heard that it is in Me that you live and move and exist? I will continue to train you spiritually in My love, in My infinite measure so that your motives become those of our reflection and through your mouth I shall continue to speak and raise many of your dead.

It is The Father who sends you out travelling, I am with you though all the time. Soul! I shall continue to model you according to our image, so that when your perishable nature must perish I may lift you once again[1] to walk into our courts.

Trust Me Vassula, and allow Me to flutter freely in you; allow Me to breathe in you, so that I can continue to teach you with wisdom and counsel. Everything I do, My infant, is not of the letter but by My infinite holiness and glory. My knowledge embodies the truth. Come and possess the truth and all that I own, it is freely given to all mankind. Seek My goodness, My patience and My tolerance so that in your weakness these gifts may lead your mind and your heart to a greater repentance. Yes, live holy as I am

---

[1]That is the second resurrection.

holy... be holy in every one of your actions and do not let me flee from My dwelling place[1] for lack of holiness.

Let your loyalty to us grow as our loyalty[2] to preserve you from falling into a lethargic spirit and back into the evils of the world. Let your joy be in Us. Daughter, pray that the prophecies may be quickly completed and that I, the utter fullness of God, the utterance of your spirit, the light in your eyes, descend in your midst to show the world how wrong it was, to show to the Churches their iniquity of their division and how, although they declare daily that there is one Lord, one faith, one baptism and one God who is father of all, over all, through all and within all, are uncharitable with one another. We cannot say: "You have done everything to preserve the unity I offered you in the beginning when you were still a child[3] and in My arms. Today you say: "I am not a child any longer and I can walk by myself," and since then you stepped out of My embrace and accustomed your steps to walk your own way... Oh child of the Father! Fruit of the son! My city and My bride! Your fragrance left you.. are there going to be any survivors left in you when I will descend in full force?

I am standing at your doors knocking; if anyone of you hears Me calling and opens the door, not only will I come in to share his meal, side by side but will also engrave on their flesh My new name. They will call My name then, and I shall listen to them and I will say once more: "These are my people, a Holy Priesthood and I will live among them all."

---

[1]That is: our soul.
[2]The loyalty between the Holy Trinity.
[3]The primitive church.

Have you not heard? "All flesh is grass and its beauty like the wild flowers. The grass withers, the flowers fade, but the word of the Lord remains for ever."[1] so why do you call yourself "God" and enthrone yourself in the sanctuary? Come and repent and allow Me to guide you back into your divinity. If you allow Me to be your torch and light, no worldly law can touch you. Come and inherit our kingdom in the right spirit. Ask for My gifts and I shall give them to you: how can you say to your soul: "Soul, you have plenty of good things now, take things as they come: have a good time and roll in your wealth, obviously the inheritance is yours." Alas for your adultery! Alas for your slanderous accusations that have been made by those who walk with the outward appearance of religion but reject the inner power of the Church! They are really members of the evil one, never realising that they are a wilderness and a drought, a walking wretch, pitiably poor and naked too. How could you believe I could live in you[2] and offer you My gifts, you who are in debt to sin? Have you not read how I shun deceit?

Ah Vassula, how so few know about Me and yet it is I, who hold all things together, am everywhere and know everything to the depths of God.

Let your love grow in Me, and your joy be complete in Me so that your spirit sings praises to Me. Let your heart be in peace with Me and your spirit forgiving, bear with patience the cross entrusted to you for all you do does not go in vain. Repay wickedness with kindness, repay evil with goodness and love. Be mindful to the poor and the wretched to give glory to Me. Be loyal and trustful only to your God alone. Alone you are not. I, the Holy Spirit, am

---

[1] Is. 40:6-8.
[2] The church.

your life and the one who directs you into Our Kingdom. Pray without ceasing and be holy in My presence.

APPENDIX

BIBLIOGRAPHY

Bibliography of the mystical writings of Vassula Rydén.

<u>List of Published Books</u>:

1. The Vrai Vie en Dieu, O.E.I.L. François de Guibert, Paris, France, 1990-1994, Vol I-IV. Supplement I-V, supplement VI to appear in June 1994.
2. La Vraie Vie en Dieu, Prières de Jésus et Vassula, Paris, France, 1993.
3. True Life in God, Trinitas, Independance MO, USA, 1991, Vol I-VII. Vol VIII to appear May 1994.
4. True Life in God, JMJ Publications, Northern Ireland, 1991, Vol I; 1992 Vol II; 1993 Vol III; Vol IV to appear June 1994.
5. True Life in God, Prayers of Jesus and Vassula, JMJ Publications, N Ireland, 1993
6. Das Wahre Leben in Gott, German, Miriam-Verlag, Jestetten, Germany, 1992-1993, Vol I-IV. Vol V to appear in the course of this year, 1994.
7. La Vera Vita in Dio, Italian, Edizioni Dehoniane, Roma, Italy, 1992-1994, Vol I-VI.
8. Prawdziwe Zycie w Bogu, Polish, Vox Domini, Katowice, Poland, 1993-1994, Vol I-IV. Vol V to appear May 1994, Poland

9. Wasze Modlitwy Moga Zmienic Swiat, Prawdziwe Zcie w Bogu, (Polish prayer book), Vox Domini, Katowice, Poland 1993.

10. A Verdadeira Vida em Deus, Encontros com Jesus, Portuguese, Brasilian, Ediçoes Boa Nova, Requiao, Famalicao, Portugal, 1992-1994, Vol I-V, to appear shortly Vol VI.

11. La Verdadera Vida en Dios, Encuentros con Jésus, Spanish, Mexican, Colombian, Puerto Rican, Ediçoes Bao Nova, Requiao, Famalicao, Portugal, 1993-1994, Vol I-II.

12. Het Ware Leven in God, Dutch, Stichting Getuigenis van Gods Liefde, Eindhoven, Netherlands, 1993-1994, Vol I-II.

13. Mir I Ljubav - Pravi Zivot u Bogu, Croatian, Beograd, Makedonska. 1993-1994, Vol I-III, Vol IV to appear June 1994.

14. Igaz Elet Istenben, Jézus beszélgetései Vassulaval, Hungarian, Marana Tha sorozat 26 Kiado: Az Emmausz Katolikus Karizmatikus Közösség, Budapest, 1993, Vol I, Vol II to appear mid-1994.

15. I Alithini En Théou Zoi, Greek, Politistikos Silogos, Irini Ke Agapi, Athens, 1993, Vol I, Vol II, to appear in May 1994.

16. True Life in God, Russian, Dom Mari, Moscow, and at the Foyer Oriental Chrétien, fr Kozina, Av de la Couronne 206, Brussels, (Prophecies of Russia).

17. Het Ware Leven in God, Flemish, Mevr Lieve Van den Borre, Oostende, 1993-1994, Vol I-XVIII.

18. Sandt Liv i Gud, Danish, Niels Hvidt, Mysundegade 8/V, 1668, Copenhagen-V. 1993-1994, Vol I to appear mid-1994.

19. True Life in God, Korean, Anyang-Shi, Kyeong-gi do, 430-600, R. Spies, Center fr Damien, South Korea. 1993 Vol I, Vol II to appear mid-1994.

List of Books to appear on "True Life in God"

1. Thai: Fr Joseph Likhittham, Thailand
2. Japanese: Ms Sachiko Hitomi, Japan.
3. Arabic: J A Loussi, Bethlehem, Israel
4. Roumanian
5. Norwegian
6. Bangladeshi: Fr James Fannan, Dhaka
7. Ukranian: c/o Fr Cyrill Kozina, Brussells
8. Indonesian

Bibliography of extracts of True Life in God to appear in June 1994, in Northern Ireland

1. Fire of Love, (Teachings on the Holy Spirit), 1995, JMJ Publications, N Ireland.
2. God Comments on His Ten Commandments, 1994, JMJ Publications, N Ireland

Published books about Vassula Rydén:

1. Michael O'Carroll CSSp 'Vassula of the Sacred Heart's Passion', 1993, JMJ Publications, Belfast, N Ireland.
2. Michael O'Carroll CSSp Vassula de la Passion du Sacré-Coeur, 1993, (O.E.I.L.) F X de Guibert, Paris, France.
3. Abbot René Laurentin, 'When God gives a Sign', 1994, Trinitas, Ind, MO, USA.
4. Abbé René Laurentin, Quand Dieu Fait Signe, (Réponse aux objections contre Vassula), 1993, (O.E.I.L.) F X de Guibert, Paris, France
5. Padre René Laurentin, Quando Dio si Manifesta, 1994, Edizioni, Dehoniane, Roma, Italy.

6. Mons Aldo Gregori, Vassula Rydén, **Messaggera di Cristo o Profetessa della New Age?**   1993, Edizioni Segno, Udine, Italy.

7. Fraternidade Missionaria de Cristo-Jovem, Quem é Vassula? 1993, Ediçoes Boa Nova, Requiao, Famalicao, Portugal.

Books to appear shortly about Vassula Rydén

1. Ovila Melançon SJ, Le Christ appelle sa Messagère: Vassula Rydén, 1994 (O.E.I.L.) F X de Guibert, Paris, France, to appear April 1994.

2. Cyril Auboyeneau, Point de Vue Orthodoxie sur La Vraie Vie en Dieu, 1994 (O.E.I.L.) F X de Guibert, Paris, France, to appear June 1994.

3. Dr Philippe Loron, (neurologue), Analyse Scientifique sur La Vraie Vie en Dieu, 1994, (O.E.I.L.) F X de Guibert, Paris, France, to appear April 1994.

4. Michael O'Carroll CSSp, 'Bearer of the Light - Mediatrix of Divided Christians' 1994, JMJ Publications, Belfast, N Ireland, to appear within one month.

Articles on Vassula that appeared in various publications:

1. Michael O'Carroll CSSp, 'John Paul II, apostle of the Holy Spirit, Dictionary of his Life and Teaching' 1994, article Vassula Rydén; JMJ Publications, Belfast, N. Ireland

2. Michael O'Carroll CSSp, 'Verbum Caro.' A theological Encyclopedia of Jesus the Christ.   Liturgical Press, Collegeville, MN 1992, Article Vassula Rydén, p.189f.

3. Howard Q Dee, (Ex-Ambassador of the Vatican), Mankind's Final Destiny, Kyodo Printing Co, 1992, Manila, article Vassula Rydén, p.116.

4. Dr and Mrs Mansour, Our Lady of Soufanieh, Syrian Arab Republic, and Other Phenomena, 101 Foundation, USA, 1991, article Vassula Rydén, p.95-105.
5. Abbé René Laurentin, Comment la Vierge Marie leur a rendu la Liberté (O.E.I.L.) F X de Guibert, Paris, France, 1991, article Vassula Rydén, p.93-97
6. Abbé René Laurentin, 12 Années d'Apparitions (Dans l'horreur de la guerre, l'amour des ennemis), (O.E.I.L.) F X de Guibert, Paris, France, 1993, p.43, 44, 58, 63.
7. Alfons Sarrach, Medjugorjes Botschaft, vom dienenden Gott, 1993, Miriam Verlag, Jestetten, Germany, article Vassula Rydén
8. Jean Mathiot, Icônes surprenantes de al Mère de Dieu, Médiaspaul & Editions Paulines, Paris, France, 1990, article Vassula Rydén, p.71.
9. P Martino M Penasa, Il Libro della Speranza, (Commento al Testo dell'Apocalisse), 1989 Padova, Italy.
10. 101 Foundation, NJ, USA, Messages Pertaining to Russia and the World. 1992, article Vassula Rydén, p.1-3, 5-6, 13, 18, 22, 30.
11. Paul Bouchard, (dir of l'Informateur Catholique, Quebec, Canada), Le Règne de Dieu...au ciel ou sur la terre? 1994, several articles and pages on Vassula Rydén.

Articles in various publications (magazines, newspapers)

French (especially Chrétiens Magazine and Stella Maris), English, Greek, Italian, Portuguese, Brasilian, Dutch, Swedish, Arabic, Canadian (especially L'Informateur Catholique).

THE FOLLOWING ARE THREE PR⸍
JESUS RECOMMENDS US TO PRAY

NOVENA OF CONFIDENCE TO
THE SACRED HEART OF JESUS

O Lord Jesus Christ, To Your Most Sacred Heart I confide this intention...

(Here mention your request)

Only look upon me, Then do what Your Heart inspires... Let Your Sacred Heart decide... I count on it... I trust in it... I throw myself on It's mercy...

Lord Jesus You will not fail me. Sacred Heart of Jesus, I trust in Thee. Sacred Heart of Jesus, I believe in Thy love for me. Sacred Heart of Jesus, Thy Kingdom Come. O Sacred Heart of Jesus, I have asked for many favours, but I earnestly implore this one. Take it, place it in Thy Sacred Heart. When the Eternal Father sees it covered with Thy Precious Blood, He will not refuse it. It will be no longer my prayer but Thine. O Jesus, O Sacred Heart of Jesus I place my trust in Thee. Let me never be confounded. Amen.

PRAYER TO ST. MICHAEL

St. Michael the Archangel, defend us in the day of battle, be our safeguard against the wickedness and snares of the devil. May God rebuke him, we humbly pray, and do thou O Prince of the Heavenly Host, by the Power of God, cast into Hell Satan, and all the other evil spirits, who prowl through the world seeking the ruin of souls. Amen.

MARY, QUEEN OF HOLY ANGELS - PRAY FOR US!

THE MEMORARE OF
ST. BERNARD

Remember, O most gracious Virgin Mary never was it known that any one who fled to thy protection, implored thy help or sought thy intercession, was left unaided. Inspired by this confidence, I fly unto thee, O Virgin of Virgins My Mother! To Thee do I come, before Thee I stand sinful and sorrowful. O Mother of the Word Incarnate! despise not my petitions, but in thy mercy, hear and answer me. Amen.

NEW TITLES AVAILABLE

John Paul II - A Dictionary of His Life and Teachings by M O'Carroll CSSp

A quick and fascinating guide to the life and teachings of this outstanding leader of the Church, which will be of great help to Catholics in these confused times. What has John Paul II said about the third secret of Fatima? What does he think of Opus Dei? the Orthodox Churches? the Jews? What was his relationship with Monsignor Lefebvre? All these questions, and many more, have been answered in this book compiled by one of the outstanding theologians of our day, Fr Michael O'Carroll CSSp, Blackrock College, Dublin, Ireland.

Bearer of the Light by M O'Carroll CSSp

This is the second book by Fr Michael O'Carroll on Vassula and the messages 'True Life in God.' In this book Vassula's most recent visit to Russia is recorded. Other themes include: pre-history of her conversion; extraordinary signs; the Passion; Chastisement and Purification. The book includes some extraordinary personal testimonies from people all around the world who experienced supernatural events in her presence. A must for any reader of the 'True Life in God' messages.

Volume IV (Notebooks 65-71)

This most recent volume of the messages of 'True Life in God' contains, among other things: prophecies on Russia explained - resurrection of the Church - repairing what was undone - unity by intermarriage. Daniel explained - the Rebel - the "enemy enthroning himself in 'my sanctuary'" - abolition of the Perpetual Sacrifice. Message to Cardinals, bishops and priests (17 March 1993).

Fire of Love

In this book prepared by Vassula Rydén from the complete works of 'True Life in God' to date are those passages she considers the most important references to and by the Holy Spirit. Note to the Reader by Emil Castro and Preface by Fr Ion Bria, Professor of Orthodox Theology, World Council of Churches, Geneva.

When God Gives a Sign by René Laurentin

Father Laurentin has long been recognised for his scientific and theological approach to claimed apparitions and his search for the truth. In this book he skillfully and with discernment answers questions arising in relation to Vassula Rydén's charism and the 'True Life in God' messages.

(This book is also available in the UK from Sue Ellis, Spring House, Spring Bottom Lane, Bletchingly, Surrey, England Tel: 0883 346365 and in the USA from Trinitas, PO Box 475, Independence, MO, USA 64051)

OTHER TITLES AVAILABLE

Prayers of Jesus and Vassula

A beautiful assortment of prayers, some given by Jesus, others by Vassula, inspired by the Holy Spirit. A section on the Devotion to the Two Hearts; Daily Prayers and quotations of Jesus' teaching how to pray.

Volume I (Notebooks 1-31)

Guardian angel Daniel, prepares Vassula to meet Jesus. Jesus teaches Vassula love of God, the scriptures; describes His passion; His love of 'daughter' Russia and its resurrection; the Great Apostasy. He links Garabandal to Fatima; His desire for unity of the Churches.

Volume II (Notebooks 32-58)

Jesus teaches that God is alive and very near, desiring a return to love, Adoration, sharing His Passion, consoling Him; return of Jesus. He teaches about the state of the Church, His shepherds; the renewal of His vineyards; Devotion to the Two Sacred Hearts of Jesus and Mary; expands on the ten commandments and Beatitudes; Apocalypse 12. The rebellion in the Church and the Great Apostasy; the suffering of His Peter; the minature judgement; unrolling of the 'scrolls.' Many prayers, of consecration, of adoration, of consolation, praise etc... to Father, Son and Holy Spirit.

Volume III (Notebooks 59-64)

Among the contents in this volume: Jesus marks foreheads with the consecration to him, Judgement Day, the time of sorting, the lamb's seal, the three days of darkness, and a strong message when the earth will shake and the sky will vanish.

Vassula of the Sacred Heart's Passion by Michael O'Carroll

A 220 page book giving an outline of Vassula's life, her charism and analysis of Jesus' messages in the light of the teaching of the Church. Also a message to cardinals, bishops and priests of 'The Rebel' with a warning not to listen or follow the teaching of anyone except the Holy Father, John Paul II. (17 March 1993)

Volume V (Notebooks 71-77)

Available in September 1995

True Life in God
Original Handwritten Version

1. 'When God Gives a Sign' (Vassula Rydén) by Rene Laurentin
2. 'My Angel Daniel' - early dawn of 'True Life in God'
3. Videos and Audios

Available from: Pat Callahan
Trinitas
Independence
PO Box 475
Missouri
USA 64051-0475
Tel: (816) 254-4489
Fax: (816) 254-1469

'True Life in God' magazine (English) available from:

Ewa Allan, Unity Publishing, PO Box 504, Bromham, Bedford MK43 8SJ, England
(Tel: 01 234 825937/ Fax: 01 234 825779)

'True Life in God' books are available in the following languages:

Switzerland: True Life in God, PO Box 902, CH-1800 Vevey, Switzerland

Phillipines: Center for Peace Asia, Shaw Blvd Cor. Old, Wackwack Road, Manduluyong Metro, Manila, Philippines. Tel: 795-622. Fax: 922-8358

French: 1.Edition du Parvis, CH-1648 Hauteville, Switzerland

2.'La Vraie vie en Dieu', Editions FX de Guibert (OEIL), 27 Rue de l'Abbé Grégoire, F-75006 PARIS

German: Das Wahre Lebe in Gott, Mariamverlag, D-7893 Jestetten, Germany

Italian: 'La Vera Vita in Dio', Edizioni Dehoniane, Via Casale San Pio V, 20, 1-00165 ROMA, Italy

Spanish/:   Centro de Difusion 'Grupo Reina', Belisario
Mexican   Dominguez 1302,"Laboratorios Jema", Mazatlan, Sin, Mexico CP 82000 Tel: (91-69) 82-11-59

Portuguese/: Ediçoes Boa Nova, 4760 Vila Nova de
Spanish: Famalicao, Famalicao, Portugal. Tel: 75-165. Fax: 311-594

Polish: Vox Domini, Skr Poczt 72, 43-190 Mikolów, Poland

Greek: Candy Jeannoutsikos, Essex SA, Fokionos 8 Ermou, 10563 Athens, Greece

Russian: Cyril Kozina, Foyer Oriental Chrétien, 206 Ave de la Couronne, B-1050 Bruxelles, Belgium

Korean: Father R Spies, Father Damien Center, PO Box 36, Anyang-Shi, Kyeong-Gi Do 430-600, South Korea

Flemish: Mevr Lieve Van den Berre, Epsomlaan 34, 8400 Oostende, Belguim. Tel: (059) 503-752

Danish: c/o Niels Christian Huidt, Louis Petersenveg, 2960 Rungsted-Kyst, Denmark

Bangladeshi: Father James Fannan, National Major Seminary, Plot 9, Road No.27, Banani, Dhaka 1213, Bangladesh

Indonesian:	Indriati Makki, Jalan Larong no.1a, Kompleks PLN, Kelurahan Duren Tiga, Jakarta 12760, Indonesia
Norwegian:	Ingfrid Lillerud, Lerdalsvn 22, 1263 Oslo, Norway
Ukranian:	Cyril Kozina, Foyer Oriental Chrétien, 206 Ave de la Couronne, B-1050 Bruxelles, Belgium
Dutch:	Stichting Getuigenis van Gods Liefde, PO Box 6290, 5600 HG Eindhoven, Holland
Bulgarian:	Miladora Anastassova, Bd D Grover 20, 1606 Sofia, Bulgaria
Hungarian:	c/o Ilma Jordan, Szolyva v 1/b, 1126 Budapest, Hungary
Croatian:	Franjo Ereiz, Za Belaka, Za M D Vukić, Palmotićeja 33, 41001 Zagreb PP699, Croatia
Japanese/ Chinese:	Serge Bernard Kuhn, Foyer de Charite, Ai to Hakari no Ie, Sendaiji 136, Oaza, 568 Ibaragi-Shi, Osaka-Fu, Japan
Canada:	Caravan Agencies, 6 Dumbarton Blvd, Winnipeg, MBR3, P2C4 (Tel: 204 895-7544/ Fax: 204 895-8878)

Queries relating to any version, please contact:

Patrick Beneston
Association la Vrai Vie en Dieu
5 Rue de Turbigo
75001 PARIS
France

(Fax: France [1] 34-93-08-13)

NATIONAL DISTRIBUTORS (ENGLISH EDITION)

United Kingdom

Chris Lynch
JMJ Publications
PO Box 385
Belfast BT9 6RQ
United Kingdom
Tel: (1232) 381596
Fax: (1232) 381596

Australia

Center for Peace
c/o Leon LeGrand
91 Auburn Road
AUBURN Victoria
Australia 3123
Fax: (03) 882-9675
Tel: (03) 882-9822

United States

John Lynch
PO Box 533
Bethpage
N.Y.
USA 11714-0533
Fax: (516) 293-9635
Tel: (516) 293-9635

Philippines

Mary and David
PO Box 146
Lapulapu City 6015
Cebu
The Philippines
Fax: (6332) 310305

South Africa

Winnie Williams
Friends of Medjugorje
PO Box 32817
Braamfontein 2017
Johannesburg
South Africa
Tel: (011) 614-3084
Fax: (011) 614-3417

Republic of Ireland

D.M.Publications
"Maryville"
Loughshinney
Skerries
Co Dublin

Tel: (1) 8491458
Fax: (1) 8492466

Malawi

Rui Francisco
PO Box 124
Lilongwe
Malawi
Africa

Fax: (265) 721504

Denmark:Niels Huidt, Mysundegade 8V, DK 1668, Copenhagen
V, Denmark (Fax: 45 331 33115)
Switzerland: Parvis, CH-1648, Hautville, Switzerland (Tel: 41 29
51905)
Holland:Stichting Getuigenis, Jan Van Hooffstraat 8, 5611 ED
Eindhoven, Holland (Tel: 040 43 39 89 Fax: 040 44 02 74)

Manual of Office-Based
Anesthesia Procedures